Born Dec. 4, 1916
died Sept. 13,
2007

Rcd.
Feb. 20, 2002

Happy trails!
Robin Earl Chlupach W

2/15/02

To: Joe & Dick Scott: Fairbanks
This Promised
Land to met.
assume
a

Sept. '07
We are happy
to give this host
and letters from
Augie & UAF. It
was our privilege to
finally meet him
in 2002. Sincerely,
Dick & Jo Scott

Sept 11, 2005 - We had
another gathering to honor
Augie when he was in
Jbks. for the ribbon cutting
of new museum on Sat.
Sept. 10,
Jo Scott

June 15, 2002
Gathering in home of
Dick and Jo Scott to honor
Augie. About 50 people
came — beautiful morning.
Touching testimonials. Jo

AIRWAVES
OVER
ALASKA

AIRWAVES OVER ALASKA

The Story of Broadcaster Augie Hiebert

As told by his daughter

ROBIN ANN CHLUPACH

Foreword by

WALTER CRONKITE

SAMMAMISH PRESS
ISSAQUAH, WASHINGTON

DEDICATED

to his grandchildren . . . and theirs.

As he has set a good example throughout his life for his family and others, may his future generations gain strength from his perseverance and determination to pursue and fulfill his dreams in a manner uncompromising of his principles. May his future generations meet the challenges of life with the courage of commitment, and may they always maintain a sense of humor, remembering the "twinkle in his eyes."

CONTENTS

Foreword by Walter Cronkite
7
Preface
11
Acknowledgments
13
Introduction
15

Chapter 1: Apples, Apples, Apples! 17

Chapter 2: Under the Midnight Sun 33

Chapter 3: Through the Magic Window: the 1950s 83

Chapter 4: Stormy Weather: the 1960s 115

Chapter 5: Beam Me Down, Scotty! 147

Chapter 6: The Thrill of Victory: the 1980s 193

Appendix
213

FOREWORD

Walter Cronkite

N ow I had a lot of my upbringing in Texas, and so I sort of had a feeling that wasn't quite right about Alaska coming into the Union. For all those years of my youth, Texas, if it had nothing else, had the claim of being the nation's largest state. Alaska squashed that once and for all.

And, another thing—I never was particularly fond of cold weather. Oh, I could take it all right and as a kid enjoyed sledding down the steep hills of my native Kansas City, Missouri—the other place of my childhood. But as I grew older, in Texas, there wasn't much opportunity for winter sports, and by the time I was ready to try skiing, I found the trouble of all that gear you had to get into more annoying than the fun I got out of it. (That was when I decided that I liked sports in direct relation to the number of clothes you take off to do them.)

So Alaska didn't have a lot of lure for me as a winter wonderland either. My only experience with the state was at one airport or another, and I never could remember whether it was Nome, Fairbanks, Anchorage, or some other place where you had to stop to refuel on some of those early transpacific flights.

Were my eyes opened a couple of years back when Pat and Augie Hiebert gave my wife, Betsy, and me the grand tour of the state of which they are so proud!

They took us from one end of that vast land to another. We saw the beginning of the great pipeline up on the North Slope, and we visited the end of it at Valdez where the tankers engorge the oil pouring down from that frozen treasure house.

We saw the magnificence of the mountains and even rode a small ski plane up to the climbers' base camp on the slopes of Mount McKinley. Our pilot-host on that trip was Lowell Thomas, Jr., as fascinating and delightful a character as his famed father. He operates the base camp and the air service that supplies it.

We had our awe inspired by the great glaciers and by the crenelated shore of the southern coast. We were intrigued by the old Russian community of Sitka.

We visited Homer and a little cove outside town which we agreed was about as beautiful a spot as we ever had visited in all our travels around the world. (We also agreed not to mention its name in public because the folks who live there hope to stave off as long as possible the pressure of development. That is a dim hope, but I'm not going to give them cause to point a finger at me when it happens.)

There, as elsewhere, we met and were mightily impressed by the spirit of the Alaskans. The population across all those square miles is sparse, indeed, and neighbors are sometimes far apart. The isolation brings a converse closeness. As it once was on our Great Plains (and still is, thank goodness, in some corners of our nation), neighbors help each other.

A sterling example came to our knowledge on that wonderful cove: The sprawling home of one of the most popular inhabitants, a leader of the community, one windy, wintry day was consumed in a terrible fire that claimed the life of the youngest family member, a small child. That afternoon while some of the debris still glowed hot, the neighbors began clearing the site. In the ensuing weeks, they bent to their job. They dropped their own schedules to put full time into the project. And they rebuilt the house.

We traveled to the far western edge of Alaska, and in the little native village of Kotzebue, facing the Soviet Union not so far away, we were given a dinner by the local residents. They had told us that the evening was strictly informal, but they themselves broke out their finery. The men kidded each other until I got the distinct impression that the dress shirts, neckties, and business suits they were wearing were rare habit in Kotzebue.

It was a cozy, warm, and friendly dinner, and afterward the head man made a little speech. "We aren't a very rich village," I remember him saying. "We don't have very much here. But in honor of your visit we want to give you something to remind you of our most precious possession." And he handed me a small package.

I unpeeled the gift wrapping and inside was a simply framed six-by-nine inch blowup of a snapshot. The picture was of the children of the Kotzebue school—their most precious possession indeed.

I was so touched that my thank you choked in my throat and I had to sniff away a tear. I've been to a lot of banquets in halls of state around the earth, and on a few occasions I've been presented with gifts of gold or silver or crystal. Most of them are packed away somewhere, out of sight and out of mind, but hanging in a prominent place in our home is the gift of which we are proudest—that precious possession from Kotzebue, Alaska.

When I think of those people at the far reaches of the

North Slope, and out west of Kotzebue, and down on the little cove near Homer, I know what Augie Hiebert has meant to them. He, as much as any single person, has brought them into touch with one another and with the great outside world. He was one of the pioneers who brought them radio, and now television, and it is fitting that this book by his daughter should honor his contribution to a state which I have decided deserves to be the nation's biggest, and where I probably wouldn't even mind going out in the winter.

PREFACE

This book is the story of a champion, a hero—my hero. It is not only a litany of accomplishments, but a personification of the man who served as catalyst and driving force behind the successful implementation of telecommunications in Alaska.

When I look at a painting, I see "flat," enlivened by interpretation and imagination. When I look at an object, I see dimension, enriched by its utility. When I look at a human being, I see facets molded by experience, environment, and heredity into personality and character. When I look at Dad, I see an ordinary human being. When I look at his achievements in telecommunications in Alaska, for Alaskans, I see an extraordinary man. That we Alaskans take radio and television for granted is Augie Hiebert's reward for a life dedicated to promoting its growth and quality.

In his public service to his community and to his state, the pot of gold at the end of his rainbow has been people—the people he has touched, and those who have reciprocated in kind.

Radio and television signify for me the constant and vivid immortalization of my dad. There is no other way to characterize the experience of having reconstructed seventy years of his life.

ACKNOWLEDGMENTS

Many people have contributed to the content of *Airwaves over Alaska* and supported its merit. My gratitude to them transcends expression.

Melissa's paternal grandparents graciously donated many hours of their vacation time to help me launch my project. Their generosity is much appreciated.

My sisters' support has added a new dimension to our mutual admiration society. Your energy and strength have enveloped my spirit. A special thanks to Cathy whose nimble fingers produced flawless copy of many hours of transcribed tape.

Mother has redefined the meaning of motherhood. Thank you for being there when I needed you.

Dad's patience never waned through many hours of taping. Your endurance and candor are appreciated. Thanks for being you.

There are two special people in my life who deserve credit for their inspiration and encouragement—my husband and daughter. Your love sustains my very being.

In memory of those with whom I would like to have met. May they rest in peace.

INTRODUCTION

Size, demography, topography, and Mother Nature provided a challenge to those who have dedicated their lives to broadcasting in Alaska. The evolution of communications systems in Alaska—from delivering mail by dog team to teleconferencing to live via-satellite news and sports television coverage—are historically significant.

Communication has had an impact on Alaskan history second to no other development. The broadcast media, as an integral component of communication in Alaska, has furnished Alaskans not only with quality entertainment, but enhanced the range of our educational, medical, marketing, and political capabilities.

One man, Augie Hiebert, stands out for his pioneering achievements in broadcasting in Alaska. This is his story.

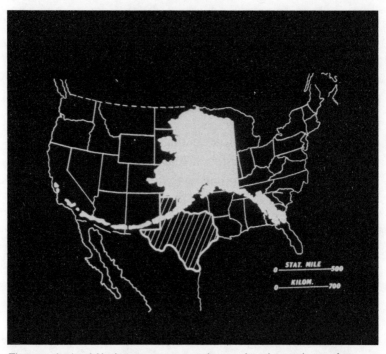

The magnitude of Alaska's vastness superimposed on the contiguous forty-eight states. Her size is only one aspect of the communication challenge. Alaska's incongruity in space and distance from the Continental U.S. has posed as great a challenge to the broadcast media.

CHAPTER 1

APPLES, APPLES, APPLES!

P eter Hiebert loved dramatics and he was good at it. During his summer breaks from acting school in Chicago, he worked in Calgary, Canada, farming wheat and raising Percherons, a breed of powerful rugged draft horse. He had homesteaded this land made available as a result of the Canadian Pacific Railroad's need to develop the area for crops to haul.

The cold Chicago winter of 1911 was warmed by his introduction to Josephine, the only child of August Moench. Josephine's mother had died shortly after giving birth, so Josephine was raised within a sheltered environment by her dad and his family. August was a successful entrepreneur in the chocolate delivery business.

On February 5, 1912, Peter and Josephine were married. Around the same time the following year they were blessed with baby daughter Margaret, and August became a granddad.

During the next couple of years, August was influenced by an advertisement luring people to "own your own farm in the west." Possessing the spirit of pioneer adventure, August agreed to the terms of the agrarian promoters, and Josephine, with her unyielding bond to her dad, chose to go with him. Peter, though hesitant to pursue a livelihood in fruit farming, had little choice but to accompany his family, his acting dreams now but a memory. In this new land, the fertile valley of Crescent Bar on the banks of the Columbia River in Eastern Washington, Peter and Josephine's second child, Augie, was born on December 4, 1916.

Once Peter had settled in and saw the opportunities for acquiring land, his penchant for accumulating real estate flourished. His love for the land was genuine, though he was a reluctant farmer. Denied opportunities for dramatic expression, he became introspective, without desire to communicate or demonstrate feelings of fondness. He worked hard all his life, loved his family, and died with his boots on.

For Josephine, the farm life was equally as difficult. It was hard work; there was no other way. Everything was done by hand. During the summer, water from the Columbia River was used to irrigate the fields and to supply running water to the house, but during the rest of the year, water had to be hauled from a nearby well. There was no refrigeration, making food preparation more difficult.

August was the only family member who realized the fruits of his dreams. Though his farm was small, he managed it well and made money.

Peter owned a 160-acre orchard—apples mostly, with a family vegetable garden, chickens, and a cow. Augie, who was called Sonny during his early years, knew early on what farm chores were all about. Learning to feed the chickens came first. Then he was groomed to work the harvest and to milk Goggles. Sonny's innate discipline and desire to work were diminished by a severe case of hay fever. To make matters worse, Goggles loved to swish her tail in Sonny's face when he was milking, and just when the pail was full, she would stick her foot in it or kick it over.

When Sonny was about eight, he learned to drive the

tractor that pulled the spraying machine used to control worm infestation in the orchard. He also irrigated the orchard, thinned the apples to promote growth, and propped up fruit-laden tree limbs to prevent breakage.

The early soft fruit crops—cherries, apricots, and peaches—brought a premium price, but raising apples was often a losing proposition. They had to be sprayed, irrigated, picked, and taken to market. All too often a box of apples brought in fifty cents less than it cost to grow them.

At school, Sonny was a good and enthusiastic student. Often he would finish his schoolwork before anyone else, and his first-grade teacher, Doady Jordan, would assign him to tutor fellow classmates in need of extra help. This not only kept Sonny out of trouble and motivated, but also helped a nineteen-year-old teacher in charge of four grades in a two room school.

Sonny was the middle child of three. Margaret was four years older, and Dick six years younger. One result of the age differences was that the children had few common interests. Normal sibling respect and camaraderie blossomed later in life.

Between the ages of eight and ten, Sonny had a number of illnesses and mishaps, some that left permanent physical damage. One spring day, Sonny and a friend were walking home from school together. As they approached the friend's house, the family dog ran out and bit Sonny on the left thigh. The bite was deep enough to expose the main artery in Sonny's leg. It is difficult to determine which pain was worse—the bite itself, the iodine poured directly onto the wound, or the subsequent rabies shots. Since the threat of rabies was constant in that part of the country, the dog's head was sent to a lab for analysis. The test was positive, and for the next two weeks little Sonny was driven every day to Dr. Vale's office in Quincy for a painful injection.

Shortly thereafter, Sonny became quite ill. The whole community was certain that the Pasteur treatment had failed and that poor young Sonny had contracted the fatal disease. But he didn't have rabies—it was only diphtheria!

War games behind the school house at Trinidad were popular for awhile. The older kids constructed a couple of forts and decided that a war with rocks would be appropriate. The little kids joined in, choosing up sides and gathering small rocks unlikely to cause injury. It was the broken brick, from the older boys' arsenal, that connected with Sonny's face, shattering his entire right cheekbone. His dad loving massaged the bulging, disfigured face back to shape, but the damage, though not readily apparent later on, was permanent. Drainage from the tear duct in Sonny's right eye was affected, as was nerve paralysis to the right side of his mouth.

Baseball and bicycles are boys' best buddies, especially within the open space freedoms of summers on a farm. For Sonny, these favorite sports also spelled disaster. The newly blacktopped country road was perfect for a young boy and his bicycle. But Sonny made the unforgivable mistake of tying a rope to a car so he could be towed on his bike. The result was a permanent blacktop tattoo on his left elbow. Sixty years later, after experiencing numbness in his left arm and fingers, he required surgery to repair degenerative nerve damage, a result of the bicycle accident.

And Sonny was the catcher one summer day when he crouched too close to the batter, and the bat made contact with his nose. Again, in later life surgery was needed to reconstruct the broken nose and mishealed nasal passages.

Sonny survived his boyhood in spite of himself. Now a mature youth, having outgrown his childhood nickname, Augie entered Quincy High School. His teenage years were filled with basketball, baseball, and ham radio—and the Depression.

The hardest part of the Depression for Augie was seeing how hard everyone had to work, particularly his dad who was in constant desperation to save what he owned. When Peter's small loan at the bank could not be paid, the bank foreclosed on the 160-acre farm and the house at Crescent Bar where Augie was born and raised. Peter also lost his section (640 acres) of wheatland in Calgary and a section of wheatland he had acquired in Quincy. It was a real blow. The Hiebert family was forced to relocate to their unencumbered smaller orchard on the back street of town. The old farm house there was renovated and life went on, as Peter began driving the ten-mile school bus route from Crescent Bar to Quincy High School.

Morgan Owings, superintendent of schools and coach of the Quincy High School basketball and baseball teams, had a lasting influence on Augie. He impressed upon his teams the importance of good conditioning; because they had so few players, each member had to play most of the time. In his junior year Augie played on a five-man basketball team; when he was a senior, the team had one substitute. Owings was inspirational in his opposition to smoking and drinking, and Augie kept the slate clean on both accounts. At 5'7" Augie was better suited for baseball than basketball, and he found his niche as a smooth-fielding shortstop. With his focus throughout high school on sports and schoolwork, Augie was honored as valedictorian of his graduating class of 1935, a class of eight.

Three years prior, in April 1932, fifteen-year-old Augie had acquired his ham radio license. He was now identified as W7CBF. His curiosity about electronics, which would eventually free him from farm life, had been piqued by his friend, Page Spencer, who had been dabbling in electronics and knew something about it. Augie, Page, and neighbor Bill Chambers seized every opportunity to read and gather their materials to build receivers and transmitters. Augie gathered sets from around town to cannibalize parts. What money he needed to finance his hobby was obtained as an asparagus picker in the spring. The equipment in those days was not as complex as it is now. The tubes were simple and the circuits were straight forward.

A small shed behind the farmhouse was perfect for a ham shack. It was an uninsulated frame structure with a single boxed-in bed and a pot belly stove—a retreat and haven. There Augie wound his own power transformers and constructed the racks to store all his equipment. His antennas meandered from the shack to poles strategically placed throughout the back yard. It was a low power operation, not very sophisticated, but it worked.

The process of learning, practicing, and perfecting international Morse code required a bit of ingenuity. The telephone system in town was just a party line; everybody was on it. Hiebert's ring was a short and a long, while Chambers's was a long and a short. The boys decided they could connect their code oscillators into this system to transmit code back and forth. It was a clever idea that proved unpopular with the town folks. The boys were soon chased off in no uncertain terms.

Shortly thereafter a barbed wire fence that almost connected the Hiebert farm and the Chambers farm was found to solve the problem of code transmission. Where the fence ended, wire was inserted to complete the connection and open their wordless world of transmission. Once they were licensed to transmit, they could hone their code speeds as well as talk to other hams.

The time following high school graduation was tough for Augie. He was torn by a desire to help his dad on the farm, versus the desire to go out on his own. His granddad's encouragement, both financially and emotionally, proved invaluable. August recognized his grandson's love of and aptitude for electronics, and enrolled him in an electronic's correspondence school. Home study lasted about a year. In February of 1938, Augie then departed for Los Angeles for three-and-a-half months of required classroom study.

Augie landed his first radio job at station KPQ in nearby Wenatchee, Washington, that summer. The federal government had recently established the wage and hour law, which meant that anyone working over forty hours per week had to be paid for overtime. KPQ had only two announcer/ engineer employees. To avoid having to pay overtime, station management decided to hire a third person to work straight time along with the original two employees. Augie was hired initially to fill in for a vacationing engineer; if things worked out, he would then slip into the "third person" slot. Two weeks was all it took. Augie's engineering skills did not fail him, but his voice did. It wasn't that he hadn't tried. While living in Wenatchee with his sister and brother-in-law, he would read aloud from Margaret's *Ladies Home Journal* and anything else he could get his hands on. Even so, he butchered copy, advertisers complained, and the station lost business. He was fired from his good paying $120-a-month job.

The ignominy was terrible. He returned home to the orchards, helping with the harvest and working in the packing sheds. Every day at home was filled with the frustration of his recently thwarted ambitions and his "imprisonment" on the farm. Then an announcer/engineer job opened up in Longview, Washington. The bus trip down proved fruitless; again it was the applicants with "pear-shaped tones" who made the grade.

In the fall of 1938, Augie heard about an announcer/engineer job with a radio station being built in Bend, Oregon. The job paid a meager $60 a month, which no self-respecting engineer would work for, but he took it. Stan

Bennett was chief engineer and Frank Loggan was station manager. Augie helped Stan build KBND, owned by the *Bend Bulletin*, a local newspaper. Frank, a newspaper man, was tapped to manage the station, which he did with a firm hand.

The question uppermost in Augie's mind was what would happen once the station went on the air and his shortcomings as an announcer were revealed. Two things worked in Augie's favor when KBND went on the air December 28, 1938, as Oregon's eighth station. First, he avoided announcing as much as possible. He worked traffic, typed logs, and even worked sales. Second, Frank Loggan was a financially astute manager. He knew if he lost Augie, he would have to hire two people to replace him. So Augie stayed on at Bend and made many friends quickly, having been accepted by the community in spite of his announcing.

In June 1939, Stan Bennett left KBND to build KFAR radio in Fairbanks. Augie then became chief engineer at KBND at a salary of $125 a month. Shortly thereafter he received a telegram from Stan saying he needed help building the station in Fairbanks. Would Augie be interested in coming up for $185 a month? Augie had survived the announcing dilemma, mostly by evasion, and was now chief engineer, but he was enamored with the idea of "building." At the age of twenty-two Augie needed some advice, and he got it from his friend the druggist.

"Who are you going to work for?"

"A man by the name of Capt Lathrop."

"I'd take the job."

"Do you know Mr. Lathrop?"

"No, but I know of him, and he's the kind of man I'dwant to work for."

The druggist then related that he was once on a boat with Capt Lathrop headed for Alaska. Along the way, someone accused the purser of stealing. Everyone except

Capt believed the purser was guilty. Capt knew the purser from the many trips he'd taken, had confidence in him, vouched for him, and ultimately saved his job. They found out later that someone else was the thief and the purser was not guilty. The druggist was compelled to believe that Capt Lathrop was a man of indisputable character to defend another human being with such determination.

On August 13, 1939, Augie arrived home in the '29 Model A roadster he had acquired in Bend during his recent, more affluent days as chief engineer at KBND. The car, dubbed Patty Jean, was turned over to his brother Dick, and two days later Augie was off to the land of ice and snow and igloos.

Two-year-old Sonny helps with farm chores.

Sonny gives Grandpa Moench a break.

Sonny and his dad use a tractor to disc the apple orchard.

Sonny with "friend," Goggles.

Augie (far right) with his junior-year high school basketball team
and coach Morgan Owings.

KBND radio staff at Bend, Oregon, taken for opening day publicity in
December 1938 (Augie in front, far right).

Black Rapids Lodge on the way to Fairbanks from Valdez.

Tripod form of communications in Alaska in 1939.

Motorcoach taken from Valdez to Fairbanks
on one-lane Richardson Highway in 1939

CHAPTER 2

UNDER THE MIDNIGHT SUN

Author's note: In early April 1987, Stanton D. Bennett (September 28, 1916 to June 3, 1987) was kind enough to spend two remaining days of his life helping me prepare this account of my dad's life. I dedicate this chapter to his memory, and in recognition of his outstanding foresight in bringing Augie to Alaska!

The week long voyage from Seattle to Valdez aboard the Baranof was pleasant and mostly uneventful. After overnighting in Valdez, Augie boarded a small bus that took him up the old, one-lane Richardson Highway to Fairbanks.

Black Rapids Lodge was immediately across the river from the galloping glacier, which then was very active. Everyone thought the bus driver was kidding when he warned, "When you get to the Lodge, keep yourself pretty well packed. If you hear a bell ring, you've gotta grab everything real fast, get on the bus and we'll go up the highway. This glacier may break loose and come across the river overnight. It's advanced eight miles this year and could come across the river any time."

That evening, while they all dined on what they

thought was a choice cut of beef (they later learned it was moose), the phone rang. There were two phones on the wall, and Sue Ravelle, the lady who ran the lodge, answered one phone, then rang the other. Augie had just witnessed a human relay system from Valdez to Fairbanks. A two-wire system on tripods ran from Valdez to a phone at Black Rapids; a one-wire grounded system ran the northern leg from a phone at Black Rapids to Fairbanks. It was impossible to connect the two systems by wire. Sue Ravelle's voice successfully linked the two together and relayed messages back and forth. This was Augie's first exposure to the state of telecommunications in Alaska in August of 1939.

Alaska was a territory and Ernest Gruening was governor. KFAR, the first radio station in Fairbanks, was built and backed by Captain Austin E. Lathrop. Capt, as he was affectionately called, was a millionaire industrialist—the "richest man in Alaska." Born in Lapeer, Michigan, in 1856, he had built up a profitable business in Ashland, Wisconsin, by the age of twenty-one. In 1889 he moved to Seattle, where during the gold rush to Alaska he purchased half interest in a schooner. His transportation business in Alaska waters fared well. It was as master of his schooner that he earned the title "Captain."

Miriam Dickey, his executive secretary, inspired the concept of radio in Fairbanks. She had worked part-time at a radio station in Seattle prior to her arrival in Alaska and perceived radio as a means to break the isolation barrier of this interior Alaskan community. In spite of much prodding, Miriam failed to convince Capt of the idea until she appealed to his sentimental sensitivities for Alaska and her people. Why not build a radio station as a living memorial? she asked. Capt had on occasion been approached to finance temporal monuments in memory of this or that, but radio would be a legacy left for all. And so it was to be . . . Midnight Sun Broadcasting.

Capt was tough; his language was likened to that of a mule skinner. But he cared about people and he cared about Alaska. He was a fair man. His employees were his family; for them he would do anything. Capt had the foresight to do things right in Alaska, and he had a lot of money to pursue what was within those sights. What he earned in Alaska, he gave back to Alaskans in quality projects—buildings, theaters, radio stations.

Fairbanks, situated at the geographic center of Alaska, was the third largest city at the time. It has continued to be the hub of interior Alaska. The population then was thirty-three hundred with a trading area of eight thousand people. Mining, principally gold mining, was the chief industry. Capt Lathrop's Healy River Corporation, a successful coal mining operation, was a labor-intensive industry supplying the high energy demands of gold mining. The interior railroad was built specifically to move coal to the gold dredging sites. Dairy, lumbering, and fur trapping were also vital industries. The University of Alaska offered degrees in mining, civil engineering, and forestry.

Fairbanks was, and remains, a friendly town in the middle of nowhere, the heart of an extensive outlying area. Because there was little entertainment, hospitality was prevalent and people knew each other well. Card and board games, such as the just introduced Monopoly, were popular during the long, cold winters, as were organized dances, skiing, and sledding—anything to stave off cabin fever!

Cabin fever was intensified by people's isolation from family and loved ones in the Lower 48. There were no phone lines from Alaska to the outside. The Alaska Communication System (ACS) used Morse code to relay messages from Seattle to Juneau to Anchorage to Fairbanks. It took several hours for even a short message to reach its final destination. Mail service was by steamship which meant over a week for postal delivery. In 1940 Pacific Alaska Airways (later Pan American) began once a week flights with a ten-passenger Lockheed Electra. Pilots were fair-weather fliers since instrumentation was nonexistent. A system of radio relays was therefore established between Seattle and Fairbanks for air guidance control. News and sports reports, given the communication handicap, were unreliable and therefore frustrating. So when radio came to Fairbanks, it was truly a red-letter day.

A radio station in a town of less than ten thousand was unheard of. For that size market, a station with a broadcast signal between 100 to 250 watts was appropriate. When first built, KFAR was a 1,000-watt station. That was the way Capt Lathrop did things. He built the best with the best, sparing nothing to ensure quality in construction or comfort for his employees.

Capt had a keen sense about construction. His innovative ideas were precursors to modern construction techniques. Capt built the first concrete-reinforced building in Fairbanks, the Empress Theater. Until then, everything had been wood frame. It was thought that concrete would never withstand the destructive effects of permafrost. The Empress Theater stands today as the Co-Op Drug in Fairbanks, having endured not only the permafrost, but downtown fires which leveled adjacent frame buildings. Capt later built the first concrete building in Anchorage, also called the Empress Theater, which withstood the 1964 earthquake, while others nearby collapsed. Capt believed that if he built a good quality building, it would require less maintenance. Seeing wisdom in this philosophy, the federal government followed suit shortly thereafter with the first complete concrete structure in Fairbanks, the Federal Building which housed the U. S. post office.

Jim Wallace, chief engineer at KVI radio in Seattle,

was a consultant in radio construction. Capt contracted him to build KFAR, giving Jim unlimited authorization to procure whatever resources were needed to build the first radio station in Fairbanks and the northernmost station in Alaska. The FCC license was applied for and granted, and Stan Bennett was hired out of Bend, Oregon, to engineer the project. This was in July 1939.

Stan, knowing his work was cut out for him, meticulously planned and ordered equipment, under constant logistical limitations. By August it was evident that he would need extra help to complete the project by mid-September to early October. Stan trusted Augie's engineering resourcefulness and requested that he be hired.

Radio was a mystery to Capt, and he had great respect for those who understood the technical aspects of it. Capt's reaction when he first met Augie was unforgettable—Augie looked more like a schoolboy than a capable radio engineer. Capt just couldn't believe that Augie knew all that he would soon demonstrate as a professional. Thereafter Capt would look at Augie and shake his head.

By the time Augie had arrived in Fairbanks, August 23, 1939, Stan had already completed most of the transmitter installation. The transmitter itself was in, as were a couple of the auxiliary racks, but they had not yet been wired. Augie's first job was to wire the racks and to build rhombic antennas used to pick up short-wave news.

In addition to basic logistical problems, Alaska provides many unique broadcast challenges. One of the initial problems to overcome was fade-outs caused by magnetic storms. To help solve this problem, they consulted Dr. Lloyd Berkner at the University of Alaska. Dr. Berkner was on a one-year assignment at the university to install an auroral research ionosphere station to measure the height of ionized reflecting layers. The transmitter, which Stan and

Augie dubbed the "Ya-Hoodi," scanned the broadcast band from 540 Khz clear up to 15,000 Khz every fifteen minutes, transmitting signals that would reflect back from the ionosphere. A series of measurements had been completed that told how high the layer was and gave an indication of ideal frequencies needed to transmit and receive signals. It was enough information for Stan to design the specialized rhombic antennas. This included the planting of eight telephone poles with elaborate wiring to the antenna system. One of the 850 foot antennas pointed toward New York, while its twin was directed toward San Francisco. The two antennas were linked to a specialized receiver to create dual diversity reception which combined to reduce fading.

At that time it was possible to select your own radio call letters, and a community-wide competition was held to name the new station. KFAR was selected as the winner, the call letters standing for "Key For Alaska's Riches." The station adopted the slogan, "From the Top of the World to You."

The Daily News Miner, also owned by Capt Lathrop, covered the construction progress of the new station with frequent news updates and photographs.

It was of no concern to Capt whether the radio station was a money-making proposition. The venture for him was philanthropic. He selected an experienced and capable staff, provided the environment for them to work effectively, then left them alone to do the job. Working for Capt was an unequaled opportunity. The staff at KFAR were free to produce a diversity of programming to meet the needs of the community and to fill the void in communications. That versatility was exemplary of a bygone era; contemporary specialization is a function of a highly competitive and commercialized world.

KFAR went on the air October 1, 1939. One of Augie's first station duties was to copy press. Fairbanks and the rest of Alaska had no teletype news service, such as the Associated Press or United Press International, because there were no shortwave circuits and no land lines in existence for these services. KFAR subscribed to the news service Trans Radio Press, and the main schedule was from New York. When there was fade-out on the East Coast, they switched to the San Francisco schedule, which served as a backup. News was transmitted in high speed code at forty to fifty words per minute.

Augie could copy, but not that fast; speed wasn't necessary for ham radio work. Stan copied press and he copied fast, but he needed relief from the drudgery and put pressure on Augie to build up his copy speed. With some reluctance, Augie finally was ready to relieve Stan at copy. They split the shifts, copying four to five hours every day to produce five daily news broadcasts.

Not many people could copy press at forty words per minute. As a radio operator for Pan American Airways, Hersch Frickey could. Not only was he a good friend, but a valuable asset to the engineers. For many years he took the relief shift for the engineers when they needed a break from their demanding work.

Bud Foster and Georg Nelson Meyers completed the initial staff. Bud was a successful radio announcer in Juneau at the time; his specialty was sports. Georg came to Fairbanks from Stockton, California, in June of 1939 to work at the radio station. Since the station was not yet completed, Capt hired him on at the *Daily News Miner* in the interim.

After the first few months on the air, it became evident that a full-time announcer was needed. Al Bramstedt, a senior at the University of Washington and a part-time announcer, heard about the announcing position at KFAR. Though he was in his final semester at the university, Al left to go to Fairbanks. Augie met him at the train station on a cold mid-January day in 1940. Rosa, Al's bride-to-be, stayed behind in Gray's Harbor to wait for a call to join him. Between then and their marriage in July, at which Augie was best man, Stan's ham radio phone patch was busy with the courtship and wedding plans.

During its first year of operation, KFAR remained short-staffed which resulted in an abbreviated broadcast day. Bud Foster signed on at 7:00 A.M., and Al Bramstedt took the 9:00 to 1:00 P.M. slot. The station then went off the air and resumed broadcasting from 5:00 to 11:00 P.M. Georg Meyers was news director, providing newscasts between 5:45 P.M. and 10:00 P.M. Recorded music was aired until midnight.

KFAR was the only station in Fairbanks. There was no competition, no rating books, so there was no anxiety about programming. The broadcast agenda—music, public service, entertainment, news, and sports—was intended to appeal to everyone and to meet the needs of the community. "Weather Permitting" was but one invaluable service KFAR provided. Aired every morning at ten, this program gave all the air taxi schedules for the entire area for that day. This permitted people, especially in the outlying areas, to plan for and rendezvous with flights carrying needed personal or business supplies. Knowing when to meet a flight of precious cargo was vital. At times it was also necessary to clear a runway of snow before the flight arrived.

At 10:30 A.M. a popular homemaking program called "Kitchen Kapers" was offered with Mary Cash as hostess. Mary's culinary advice was also popular with the KFAR staff, since the fruits of her on-the-air cooking were available for in-house sampling. "Story Hour with Jane" (Jane Runyan Maddox Acheson) had a loyal following among Alaska's children. "Amateur Night" was popular as well.

After spending his day at the newspaper, Georg Meyers went on the air with news at 5:45 P.M., with periodic updates until 10:00. To fill in between newscasts, he instituted a cultural program featuring classical music.

Live music was broadcast not only from the studio in the Lathrop Building, but also from the Empress Theater. Here was stored a magnificent theater organ which Don Adler played as an accompaniment to Al Bramstedt's poetry readings.

Many of the live productions were recorded, though not on tape, which had not yet been invented. The recordings were made using a ruby or diamond stylus to etch a sound pattern on an aluminum disc with an acetate coating. A record transcription service provided a variety of hit parade selections to the isolated area via parcel post.

"Tundra Topics" was probably the most enduring program. It was a popular evening show of messages and information about everything and anything, and it unified the interior. An illustration of the service the program provided occurred in Fort Yukon. A couple from the upper Yukon River village came to Fairbanks for supplies. They shopped at the Northern Commercial (NCCo.) for provisions and returned to their village well-stocked for the coming months. A neighbor heard the announcement over "Tundra Topics" that the NCCo. had mistakenly sold the couple treated and deadly poisonous seed potatoes. The neighbor made a hurried trip by boat to warn his friends, and found them preparing supper, a pot of potatoes simmering on the stove. The hungry and weary travelers had neglected to turn on their radio, but the message of danger had been clearly delivered via the air waves.

Bud Foster was a master at sporting event re-creations. Many local sporting events were broadcast live, but not major league baseball or even the World Series. Fairbanks loved baseball, and they were dependent on Bud to bring baseball to them "live." There were three keys to

Bud's re-creations: his props, a relay system of information, and Bud himself. A pencil striking a small piece of wood simulated the crack of the bat. A pencil striking a roll of toilet paper was the sound of the ball hitting the catcher's mitt. Crowd noise came from a recorded disc. The relay arrangement worked via Alaska Communications System (ACS). Twenty-five words or so an inning would come over the telegraph, and a runner would pick up the message from ACS each inning and deliver it to Bud. Bud knew the game of baseball, and from bits and pieces he would masterfully reproduce an entire ballgame. With his vivid portrayals you were there!

Once in the middle of a game, the wire went out and no more reports came through. Bud stalled—a rain delay here, a news report, then another rain delay. Finally the game resumed. The wire service may have failed, but Bud did not. No one ever knew if Bud's final score approximated the real one, but he kept the game going!

The motto for broadcasting in those early days could have been, "Have microphone, will travel." This included high school graduations, dances at Eagle Hall, and Winter Carnival and Dog Derby events, to name a few. Remotes were popular, sensational, and a challenge for the engineers. Nothing was transistorized; equipment was bulky and cumbersome. The successful coordinating of these events was a testament to Stan's and Augie's engineering capabilities. Augie would try anything; if it was innovative, he'd think of it.

The 1940 Fairbanks to Livengood dog race was a tough two-day event covering 165 miles. The teams raced from Fairbanks to Livengood the first day, then returned to Fairbanks the next. Departure and arrival times were kept for each day; when the last team came in, the times were added to determine the winner. The event was broadcast by KFAR, the first major sporting event and first dog race broadcast over the radio.

The Livengood races were later abandoned (presumably interrupted due to the war) and replaced by twenty-five-mile heat races within the Fairbanks area. Augie first conceived, planned, and executed the checkpoint system to follow these races, which produced a much more exciting radio broadcast. Augie positioned the checkpoints at a phone location near the trail or used a short wave radio remote. The equipment for the short wave checkpoints usually had to be hauled in by dog team. One checkpoint was the KFAR transmitter where the trail crossed at Farmer's Loop Road. Georg Meyers, stationed at the transmitter, would stand outside, wait for the teams, then run in and announce who had just gone by. Al Bramstedt, Ed Stevens, Ruben Gaines, and many other legendary announcers covered those first races. The checkpoint set-up, which provided an almost continuous account of racer's positions and times, made a real race out of it. The broadcast of dog races to this day relies on this system for up-to-the-minute coverage. Augie had made a significant contribution to Alaska's official state sport.

Prior to Augie's arrival, Capt Lathrop had built a four-story apartment building, primarily to provide good housing for his employees. The fourth floor was refurbished for utilization as the KFAR studio. The transmitter building, six miles out of town on Farmer's Loop Road, was new and beautiful. The central portion of the building housed the transmitter, while the left wing served as garage for the company's 1939 Chevy pickup truck, as well as furnace room and coal storage. In the right wing was a plush one-bedroom apartment, where Augie and Stan Bennett, Augie's mentor and friend, "batched."

The late night shift, originating from the transmitter,

was conducted by the engineers themselves, either Stan or Augie. They played records and did some announcing. These two young bachelors had never cooked in their lives, and they publicized their plight over the air. Their efforts did not go unrewarded. The regular announcers dubbed them the "Starvation Twins," and people from all over would make their way to the transmitter with all kinds of goodies and invitations for holiday feasting. Three turkey dinners one Thanksgiving was one of their larger reapings.

The "Starvation Twins" were enriched in other ways. People wanted to see the workings of this new miracle called radio, as well as the engineer's posh bachelor pad. The interest was so great that Stan and Augie kept a guestbook. Their first year eleven hundred people signed the guestbook (this in a town of thirty-three hundred). Once in a while, someone from the outlying bush area who had come into Fairbanks for supplies would take an expensive six-mile cab ride to the transmitter to thank the people who built and operated the station. This early response confirmed to those who worked there the station's importance to the people of Fairbanks and the outlying bush area.

Although Augie was considered by many to be shy and hard working, his free hours were packed with activities. When he wasn't working at the transmitter, he was kept busy in the Sourdough Dance Club, the Arctic Amateur Radio Club, and with his photography.

Sunday picnics at the transmitter with Al and Rosa Bramstedt were common, as well as blueberry picking and trips to Bram's cabin at Harding Lake. They were close friends who enjoyed fun times together; they also encouraged each other in times of need, such as Bram's "Bedroom Broadcaster" days. Ill with undulant fever and arthritis, Bram became a captive in his own home. When Augie constructed a "remote" broadcast facility in Bram's bedroom, he was able to read the evening news and "Tundra Topics" over the air. No one knew of the arrangement, but it was successful, as Bram puts it, "in saving my sanity." Later on Bram recalls how he rode to work on Augie's back up four flights of stairs to the KFAR studios.

The ski trail that University of Alaska students used passed by the KFAR transmitter building. Seizing the opportunity to meet people, Stan and Augie set up a Ping-Pong table in the garage and offered coffee and cookies. Lasting friendships were made—and Ping-Pong skills were sharpened.

That's not to say the trail was one way. The two eligible bachelors rarely resisted an opportunity to seek out fertile ground. Charlie Fowler and his wife, who lived in a cabin near the transmitter, had a five-dog team. After the two engineers had learned in a fashion to manage the team, they would often hit the trail for the University, with Augie in command of the sled and Stan on skis being pulled behind.

Augie spent many Saturday evenings with the Earlings, the Runyans, and the Shermers, three families who loved to get together Saturday nights for dinner, dancing, card playing, or Monopoly. They offered a family atmosphere to young people in Fairbanks, from engineers to university students. The Earlings practically adopted Augie into their family, and he became a brother to the three Earling sisters.

Augie was active in the Arctic Amateur Radio Club. Because communication was so vital to existence in the Territory, Alaska had more amateur stations per capita than any other part of the world. The club itself was new and active, having celebrated its first anniversary September 1, 1941. That year the AARC sponsored a radio and physics exhibit at the annual Tanana Valley Fair in Fairbanks. The exhibit was a big success, as scores of people gathered around the booth to look at typical amateur equipment. A sign proclaimed: "Personal Messages Sent Free to All Points in the United States," and messages were relayed from the fair booth to friends and relatives all over the country. A total of 268 messages were handled during the three nights of the fair.

When Augie and Stan were not copying press, by now mostly war news, they would often switch to an amateur short-wave band to see what they could pick up. Austin E. Cooley, Capt Lathrop's inventor nephew, was at the transmitter one of these times and asked if they could talk to New York. Contact with New York was made immediately loud and clear. The clear signal provided Austin the opportunity to propose a test for an experimental model of his latest invention. Austin had invented a new technique, called facsimile, for transmitting pictures and other information. Though told it would work over wire but never over short wave, he was in the process of testing and perfecting his novel development. The stage was set for one of the more significant experiments in the history of broadcast technology. An experimental license was granted to transmit fax over a 1,000-watt amateur radio unit, and the first ever fax picture was successfully transmitted by short wave across the continent from New York to Fairbanks. It took only eight to ten minutes to transmit an 8 x 10 photograph. Mail delivery still took a week. Fax figures could be transmitted not only by short wave when no other signal got through, but it turned out to be a superior method of transmission. Austin and his accomplishments in this field have remained a little known fact due to their highly significant contribution to privileged military war-time missions.

The military was particularly interested in transmitting maps via fax, and they kept a watchful eye on its development. The Office of War Information ultimately established stations all over the world, including a station in Kung Ming, China, which was eventually confiscated by the Russians. Every installation was a total success.

In the fall of 1941 the military in Alaska called upon the ham radio operators to provide an emergency network for early warning. Augie was appointed coordinator of the Aircraft Warning Service, Fairbanks Division. He worked closely with the military in supervising the organization and cooperation of northern Alaska operators from Barrow to Nome to Chicken. When war was declared, hams' "rag chewing" was shut down completely; only emergency messages were permitted.

During the war KFAR was granted permission to upgrade its power from a 1,000 watt, 610 Khz to a 10,000 watt, 660 Khz facility. The enhanced power enabled the station to transmit news and entertainment to our troops fighting in the Pacific, and to provide a navigational service to military planes in the area. Ladd Field (now Fort Wainwright) was an active contributor to the military war-time reconnaissance. The 660 Khz frequency was chosen to avoid interference with other stations in the States.

Augie was up early on December 7, 1941. It was a leisurely Sunday, so Augie was in no hurry to get to the control room. Prior to preparing for the routine fax test scheduled that Sunday, he flicked on the short-wave receiver. A drama on one of the stations captured his attention. About fifteen minutes into the program, the announcer interrupted with, "Japanese planes are bombing Honolulu, have attacked Pearl Harbor, and are bombing Hickam Field." Augie was the first person in Alaska to hear the news—two hours before the military was officially notified.

Augie rushed to the bedroom to tell Stan what he had heard. The next few moments were spent confirming, through messages received on additional stations, the

authenticity of the original news flash. Augie immediately
phoned the commander of Ladd Air Force Base, Col. Dale F.
Gaffney. In bed and unaware of the bombing, he thought
Augie was kidding. Col. Gaffney dashed over to the station to
listen to the recording made of the emergency broadcast,
then immediately contacted General Simon B. Buckner,
commanding general of the Army Headquarters for the
Alaska Defense Command at Fort Richardson in Anchorage.

All regularly scheduled programming on KFAR was
canceled that day. For the next few days the airwaves were
alive with war reports, press bulletins, and a direct account
from Manila, complete with descriptions of smoke clouds
billowing over Nichols Field and the thunder of overhead
bombers. The military and civilian defense authorities
utilized KFAR facilities to broadcast emergency preparedness
and requests for volunteer services. KFAR, along with many
other stations, converted to Armed Forces Radio
programming. Fairbanks had entered World War II on a
global scale.

Over the next two years, thirty-five live and direct
NBC broadcasts originated from KFAR. They were carried
often as a news bulletin—"We go to Alaska for a war
update"—such as when the Japanese infiltrated the Aleutian
Islands.

The *New York Sunday Times* published the following
story in its May 23, 1942, edition:

> The Japanese on Kiska Island call it "the
> cesspool of information," but to the United
> States troops on remote, cold assignments it
> is the last connecting link with civilization,
> being their primary source of news and
> entertainment. Such is the wartime role of
> one of America's more interesting and
> important stations, KFAR, in Fairbanks,

Alaska, whose enterprising manager, Wilson (Bud) Foster, was a visitor here last week. . . . Those who hope one day to have their own station might well envy Mr. Foster. Ten years ago he left Seattle to find his fortune in the north country and today he is program director, news editor, commentator, correspondent in the field and advertising salesman for Alaska's most powerful station, a station right on a major battlefront. . . . Mr. Foster said that the Tokyo stations put in a strong signal to Alaska but that few people listen to them. "Every time they want to get mad they turn on Tokyo," he said.

In mid-1942, Augie petitioned for a commission to the Signal Corps as a first lieutenant. Assuming he would become a commissioned officer, Augie took temporary leave from KFAR and spent two weeks with his family on Crescent Bar. When he returned to Fairbanks, he moved into the home of Mr. Earling whose family had been sent to Seattle for the duration of the war. The rest of that year, Augie worked nights at KFAR. During the day he helped install an aeronautical transmitter at the Municipal Airport as well as a radio communication facility for Aircraft Warning Service at Ladd Field.

By the end of the year Augie learned he had been rejected for military service. His contributions to the war effort as a civilian radio engineer were so vital that he was denied his petition. His biggest disappointment was that it took eight months of paper shuffling for the military to arrive at its decision.

Augie resumed his full-time duties at KFAR and returned to the living quarters at the transmitter. In February 1943, Stan was called to fulfill his war mission convictions in engineering research at MIT. Bud Foster left KFAR to become an NBC war correspondent. Georg Meyers joined the army to cover the war as a reporter for *Yank Magazine*.

Not only had Austin Cooley invented a successful page fax transmission system, but also the tape facsimile. Tape fax was never used anywhere else. Only four sets were built, two in Fairbanks and two in San Francisco. Fairbanks transmitted and San Francisco received. This operation was set up by the military to intercept Russian weather information to plan the strategic bombing of the Kurile Islands as part of the Aleutian campaign. The documentation was classified and vital for this purpose, as was the reactivation of K7XSB, which had been shut down, along with all other ham operations during the war.

The Russians as yet had not declared war on Japan, so the Russian weather information was privileged and not made available to the United States. The Russian weather information was therefore intercepted by the FCC Radio and Intelligence Division on College Hill. It was then fed to the 11th Weather Squadron, decoded and recoded by the highest qualified people in the military, transmitted by field wire from College over to the transmitter, and fed by K7XSB to San Francisco. Weather information was transmitted in coded groups by Augie through Austin Cooley's tape facsimile. The process was intense and laborious. The procedure lasted for about six months until the military was able to set up its own circuit. The KFAR office was intentionally oblivious to Augie's military involvement, but no doubt wondered why sometimes there was little to news to broadcast. Augie simply could not copy press and transmit the priority defense information simultaneously.

An incident of international intrigue occurred with the top secret defense transmissions. On July 15, 1943, a soldier at Ladd Field mysteriously drowned in Ballaine Lake near the KFAR transmitter. He was chauffeuring two Russian military officers at the time of the alleged accident. Years later Ed Fortier, then in military intelligence in Fairbanks and now retired editor of *Alaska Magazine*, through Augie's help has unraveled the mystery into one of blatant sabotage and murder. The American soldier was killed to prevent his witness and disclosure of the Russian tap of the field wire running from College Hill to the KFAR transmitter. Mr. Fortier's research and revelation has served not only to satisfy personal suspicions over many years, but has served the integrity of a young solder, at one time a suspected deserter from the U. S. Army. It was Augie's testimonial to a series of events that solidified for Mr. Fortier the true nature of the conspiracy.

The war interrupted just about every facet of everyone's life. But when the war ended, the clouds of destruction were replaced with renewed friendships, radio remotes . . . and Sparky!

• • •

Sparky was a legend in her own time. Acquired as a pup for companionship in late 1943, the Cocker Spaniel became Augie's constant and faithful shadow. Augie was now sole occupant of the transmitter apartment. His involvement in military transmissions was concluded, and he now had the time to train a lively puppy. Whether Augie was a good teacher or Sparky was a quick learner is of no consequence. Their partnership grew out of mutual respect and loyalty. Both were blessed with a sense of humor, curiosity, work ethic, and reserved, but charming presence. The following account, probably written sometime in 1946 by Georg Meyers, captures the spirit of Sparky and her endearment to the community of Fairbanks.

The most popular radio personality in Alaska
is a little redhead who doesn't sing songs,

make with the gags or analyze the day's news. She is Sparky, a mike-happy Cocker Spaniel that gets letters every day from grateful school teachers, relieved parents and entranced kids, and forged missives signed by amorous malamutes and jealous kittens.

Sparky is such an established fixture to early-morning listeners to KFAR (Fairbanks), America's farthest north commercial broadcasting station, that it is hard to remember that she first got on the air by accident. It came about because of the field mouse that got cold.

The mouse sneaked into KFAR's transmitting station, five miles out of the city, and, stomping snow off his feet, scrambled for the warmest corner of the building. He soaked up 1500 volts and knocked the station off the air. This was smack in the middle of a half-hour crime-curdler. If there is anything that a lonely sourdough trapper does not like to have interrupted, it is a bloody whodunit. Chief Engineer Augie Hiebert (who was solving the crime himself) worked into a lather trying to find out what had gummed the works. He went around making sparks with a screw-driver in a technical way. Meanwhile, his dog Sparky unscientifically followed her nose straight to the mouse, done to a crisp brown. In a few minutes radio crime resumed its traditionally unprofitable march.

The next morning, on a breezy program of platters and patter, Augie explained the interruption and gave Sparky full credit. Sparky heard her name mentioned and gave out with a bark that wasn't in the script. That bark was heard by kids in the Yukon, the Kuskokwim, the Fortymile and the Koyukuk. Mail started coming in the next day, and it hasn't stopped yet.

Now every morning Sparky yaps three or four times between 8:30 and 8:45 a.m. Sometimes it is in answer to a proposal of marriage from a husky sleddog in the Kuskokwim. Sometimes it is a happy birthday greeting to a three-year-old who has no dog but has a kitten but doesn't like kittens and would like to trade. Always it sounds like H. V. Kaltenborn recounting a world crisis.

The first letters were from kids. Then the parents started writing. They thanked Sparky for making it easy to get their youngsters out of bed in the morning. They all want to hear Sparky. And Sparky never speaks after 8:45. Gives the kids plenty of time to make it to school.

Then the school teachers. They had been having the usual trouble keeping the pupils interested in penmanship lessons. Now the teachers say: "Today, let's all sit down and write a letter to Sparky." On composition days, the schoolmarm's desks are flooded with essays on "Why I would like to have a puppy like Sparky." The novelty long ago wore off for Augie Hiebert, but Sparky eats it up. She has barked good morning in French,

Yugoslavian and Canadian. She barks agreement with parents' views on disciplinary problems. She chimes in with a high-frequency howl when Augie plays music with a certain shrill pitch. The kids gobble their mush in order to be hanging on the loudspeaker. House cats take refuge on top of the china closet, and pet pups chew up the rugs in anguish.

Sparky has posed for pictures wearing earphones and ogling a microphone. She has been photographed with her forepaws on the brink of the bathtub, soap and towel beside her, and her rag-rug ears pinned on top of her head. Mothers request this photo and write back that junior has never been so clean before. To remind Alaska's tykes that they must bundle up when they go out into the snow, Augie sends Sparky's fans pictures of her wearing a knitted sweater, fur mukluks on her feet and her ears in a crocheted snood.

Once Sparky gave a Saturday morning command performance in KFAR's downtown studio. The place was crammed with white, Eskimo and Indian kids. Sparky barked herself hoarse. She sat up, played dead, snapped at soap bubbles and rolled over until she was dizzy. The next day her fan mail contained more letters from adults than kids. "Please bring Sparky to the studio some Sunday," they begged. "It's hard for us to get off work on Saturdays."

When the Winter Carnival and Dog Derby resumed in 1946, on hiatus during the war, Sparky was named honorary Carnival Queen. Fans and followers contributed to her designer wardrobe with handmade sweater, mukluks, and in vogue snoods! As talent she performed her array of tricks, with Augie as her coach.

In mid-April 1945, Jack Walden arrived from Rapid City, South Dakota, to become assistant engineer at KFAR. Jack "batched" at the transmitter with Augie, until Nancy arrived a year later. She and Jack were married, and Augie was again best man.

Shortly after the war, the FCC began to allow ham radio amateurs to operate again. Augie's 1,000-watt transmitter used during the war would not tune to the 10-meter band, which was the first one on which hams were allowed to operate. Jack and Augie worked around the clock to get a new power amplifier built before the deadline date. They completed it in the nick of time, and jumped on the air the minute the deadline arrived. With 100 watts of power and the rhombic antennas (producing an equivalent signal of 1,000 watts), they made quite a flurry with hams in the States. The frenzy of hamming lasted about two weeks until a magnetic storm cut off transmission.

In June 1945, Augie's brother Dick arrived in Fairbanks, his first trip, to spend a week of his survivor leave. Dick was an officer in the U. S. Navy during the war, and his ship had been hit by a Kamikaze plane. Fortunately for Dick the pilot missed his target—the officers bridge—and hit the torpedo bay. The explosion was deafening, though after the initial shock, much of Dick's hearing was restored. The bond between the two brothers was also restored during their reunion that June.

During the war, the FCC had granted KFAR temporary authority to increase its power and change its frequency.

Knowing that this authority would soon be revoked, in the summer of 1945 Augie decided to conduct a survey to document the need for KFAR to maintain its "clear channel" status. Not wanting to travel the Territory alone, Augie set off with neighbor Charlie Fowler . . . and Sparky. The 1939 Chevy pickup with camper shell was home for the two week trip of camping and measuring the strength of KFAR's signal at different distances.

The survey revealed that due to the Arctic phenomena of very low atmospheric noise in the broadcast band, and the fact that remote villages had no electric generators that create manmade noise and receivers were quiet battery operated sets, broadcast signals of very low levels could provide good reception conditions, which was not the case in the Lower 48. That also meant that when propagation was good, stations in the Lower 48 on the same channel would interfere with and wipe out the desired Alaskan station. In the case of KFAR on the original 610 kilocycles and 1,000 watts of power, it had tremendous and useful coverage, until favorable propagation made interference from KFRC, San Francisco, on the same channel with 5,000 watts a reality which kept the KFAR signal from effectively serving the remote areas. The wartime clear channel of 660 kilocycles was not duplicated on the West coast, but only in New York by WEAF (later WNBC) operating on 660 kcs.

The purpose of the field intensity survey, needed to convince the FCC that for Alaska/KFAR to get interference-free coverage into its remote service area, it would have to be allowed to remain on a clear channel for all the reasons of wide-area coverage the FCC allowed it to operate during the war to serve the military with entertainment, and planes to home in on its interference-free signal. The field survey proved, and later convinced the FCC that:

1. The distance from Fairbanks to New York was so great that KFAR on 10,000 watts would never interfere with WEAF, which as a clear channel at that time was protected from any duplication of operation on their channel anywhere in the U.S. or its territories. Alaska could never receive a trace of a broadcast signal from any Eastern states, although many strong signals came in from Western states during the survey.

2. In addition to the distance, the East-West propagation path provided little, if any, signal transmission. Augie and Charlie didn't know it then, but later studies showed this was caused by the inability of signals to penetrate the polar magnetic zone.

3. The five hour time differential between East and West also worked in Alaska's favor. When KFAR signed off at midnight, it was 5:00 A.M. in New York, about the time WEAF signed on. There was no overlap of signals to interfere with each other. Since long-distance propagation exists only after sundown and before sunrise, the potential interference during the long sunshine hours of spring, summer, and fall couldn't exist in the first place.

The following summer, the FCC launched an investigation into the future of clear channel stations, and a hearing was called in July 1946 in Washington, D.C. Augie was sent to represent the interests of KFAR. Rosel Hyde had been a staff lawyer for the FCC and had just been appointed Commissioner. Rosel was from Idaho, the only Commissioner from the West. He could comprehend the position Augie presented, having come from an area with rural challenges of its own. Rosel Hyde and Augie hit it off right away.

Augie's testimony was impressive, and the FCC, largely through Commissioner Hyde's understanding and support, granted KFAR authority to remain on 660 kilohertz with full 10,000 watts of power. This was a landmark FCC decision. The clear channel issue itself, however, would remain unresolved for Alaskan purposes for nearly forty years.

The trip to Washington was Augie's first, and this initial contact with the FCC was crucial for representing Alaska's unique broadcast position. Augie Hiebert pioneered about every facet of telecommunications in Alaska, but his positive association with the FCC is probably his greatest contribution. The FCC respects him, and the broadcast community in Alaska credits him with this distinction. His track record speaks for itself. Early on it was established that his proposals were sensible, logical, and helped further the quality of broadcasting in Alaska.

In a February 1987 letter to Augie, FCC Commissioner James H. Quello wrote:

> I'm delighted to join your many friends in congratulating you on years of distinguished public service and on your exemplary achievements as both a broadcaster and civic-minded citizen. You have played a vital pioneer leadership role in the development and progress of broadcasting in Alaska and America. If broadcasting had a Hall of Fame, I would consider it an honor to present your name.

• • •

Bradford Washburn was the director of the Museum of Natural Science, and an expert mountain climber and surveyor. Brad came to Alaska to establish some surveying checkpoints and monuments on Mt. McKinley. These were later used as control points for the aerial photography of Alaska and even later translated into accurate geological survey maps of Alaska. Brad had set up camps on Mt. McKinley and it was the military's responsibility to resupply him. One year he had a supply drop from a C-54. The procedure of fly over and "dump supplies out the door" was successfully accomplished, as was radio remote coverage by KFAR. The next radio remote in which Augie was involved with Brad was somewhat of a "bomb." Supplies were loaded in the bomb bay of a B-17 bomber. The drop was on target— Brad's tent! One of the more exciting associated remotes involved a ground to air hookup with description of ground activity from the B-29 flying high over Mt. McKinley.

Prior to the helicopter era, the military had developed a unique system of search and rescue. Augie was the engineer recording the event along with an announcer describing what was to be probably one of the last of these rescue attempts prior to helicopter usage. It was midnight in May under a clear sunny sky. A preacher had gone down in a small plane near McGrath. A four engine C-54 towed a glider out to the remote area. The glider, with a crew of one, was dropped and cut loose to descend on its own. The downed individual was recovered and placed in the glider. A snatch line was constructed. This consisted of two poles planted a distance ahead of the glider. A line was wrapped pole to pole and back to the glider in a closed-Y configuration (picture a sling shot). The point of snatch would be the line stretched between the two poles. A pronged hook was attached to the end of a winch cable in the C-54. The process was to pay out the cable, time it so the cable would stretch out and pull out in back of the plane, gradually take up the weight of the glider and then pull it up and away to civilization. It was tricky. The glider couldn't be jerked up too fast. If the cable was payed out too fast and too far, it would come off the end of the winch and fall to the ground. A new cable would have to be brought back from headquarters. If the cable was snubbed too fast, the weight of the glider would pull down the C-54. The remote radio broadcast was a success, as was the rescue. The helicopter was an invaluable means of rescue, especially in remote areas of Alaska.

The first helicopters in Fairbanks were another opportunity for the illustrious KFAR "remote" crew to thrill the community with something new. For Augie the engineering was simple; it was only a matter of supplying a microphone line long enough to span from ground to air, while the announcer aboard the helicopter described Fairbanks from his aloft vantage point! The significance of the event was that it was the first use of an aircraft to accomplish a landline broadcast.

In November 1946 KFAR covered Task Force Frigid by radio remote. This remote was memorable in many ways. It was a new and daring military maneuver carried live by NBC, and due to circumstances beyond his control, it would be the last days of Augie's eligible bachelorhood.

It was twenty-five below zero. The military maneuver involved a cold weather parachute jump and week-long bivouac. The jump was made at McGrath's Potato Patch, twelve miles from Fairbanks. The men wore white clothes, masks over their faces to protect from frostbite on descent, and large packs for the bivouac. Ruben Gaines was in the plane and Ed Stevens and Al Bramstedt were on the ground. Ed had come to Fairbanks with Ruben. He was as distinctive in his sports re-creations as was Bud Foster. The remote was a complicated one. KFAR was an NBC affiliate station; NBC wanted the coverage because it was so unique. NBC would not tape anything, so it was fed live. The entire maneuver, as broadcast and described later by Ruben Gaines, was pretty much, "There they go; here they come." The engineering behind the scenes made the broadcast. Earle Grandison manned the ground remote, a short-wave, remote control pickup point on the ground near the jump. Augie was at the transmitter about seven miles away. He was to receive a start cue by short wave from the network from San Francisco. Then he would cue the men in the field when to start and feed the announcer's voice covering his end of the broadcast, received on a receiver in proximity of the KFAR transmitter, over his transmitter K7XSB to the South 48 live.

The timing not only had to be perfect, but all the remote receiver and transmitter facilities had to be strategically located and monitored to prevent their own conflicting interference. The national broadcast was rated by NBC, on a scale of 1-5, as a 5+!

● ● ●

Augie met Earle Grandison on October 1, 1939, at KFAR's opening day ceremony. He was just a kid, eleven years old, but with a passion for electronics. He went to all the Arctic Amateur Radio Club meetings and often visited the transmitter. Augie was quick to recognize the symptoms. So a couple of years later he asked Earle if he wanted to help out at the transmitter during his summer vacation. Augie made a deal with Earle: if Earle would mop the floors and perform various menial tasks to keep the bachelor quarters clean, Augie would teach him electronics. The terms were agreeable to both parties. Earle always told people that Augie would never ask anyone to do something he wouldn't do himself.

Augie started Earle testing tubes; then he progressed

to adjusting equipment and learning to tune high power transmitters. On Sundays together they cleaned the transmitter itself. The words never to be forgotten were: "Keep an electronic unit clean and it will work well for you!" Earle absorbed electronics like a sponge. In a short time, young Earle not only acquired his ham license but also his first class radiotelephone and second class radiotelegraph commercial licenses. Earle continued through his later teenage years to help out with the technical aspects of the radio remotes. Augie was grateful for the clean apartment. And Earle has enjoyed a life-long electronics career in avionics.

• • •

Pat Stadler was a second lieutenant nurse in the U. S. Army. Near the end of the war she was stationed aboard the hospital ship USS Hope in the Pacific. She was curious, outgoing, and adventuresome, which is probably what brought her to Fairbanks on Halloween of 1946. She worked at St. Joseph's Hospital, but was also hired to live in and help take care of Earle Grandison's father, who was terminally ill. Shortly after Earle's father died, Pat was asked to stay on; she and Mrs. Grandison hit it off right away.

Earle decided it would be a good idea for Pat and Augie to meet. Earle bundled her up in his mother's winter wear and ushered her along to watch the Task Force Frigid parachute jump. The maneuver involved a cold weather parachute jump and week long bivouac; it was twenty-five degrees below zero. When the broadcast was over, Earle and the announcers took Pat to the transmitter to warm up . . . and to meet Augie. That was the beginning of Augie's frequent calls at the Grandison's house. He never went empty handed, always bringing with him blueberry ice cream. (Not until their wedding day did Pat reveal her and Mrs.

Grandison's dislike for blueberry ice cream.)

They courted that cold winter of 1946-47, discussing in an old graveyard high above the city their hopes and dreams and future. It was quiet and peaceful there—a favorite courting spot.

On Christmas Eve 1946, a major fire destroyed the Fairbanks Telephone Exchange. Augie was the American Radio Relay League (ARRL) section communications manager for Alaska, and he immediately organized amateur radio efforts to provide communications for the people of Fairbanks. A network of amateur stations was strategically established throughout the city. Twice a day KFAR rebroadcast a check-in by each of the amateur stations to keep the public informed of the emergency network. An early test of the emergency set-up occurred when another major fire broke out in downtown Fairbanks. The network was used to good advantage for calling doctors and summoning additional help. Normal telephone service was restored five or six weeks later.

When the hardware store in downtown Fairbanks burned down on one of the coldest nights in Fairbanks history, power lines and wires serving the transmitter were knocked out. It was always well below zero when the power failed; it made it that much more of a challenge to get the diesel-driven auxiliary generator started. That night Augie and Jack were tested to the limit in an effort to keep the radio station on the air. When in doubt, engineers resort to heating the intake manifold with an acetylene torch!

When Augie finally thawed out that winter, he was married. Pat and Augie were married in Wenatchee, Washington, near his home at Crescent Bar, on March 16, 1947. Pat's sister, Mary, and Augie's brother, Dick, were their attendants at the family wedding at St. Joseph's Catholic Church. The newlyweds borrowed Dick's Mercury and spent their honeymoon visiting friends in Washington and Oregon. They reunited with Mary Cash, who now lived in Yakima, and the staff at KBND in Bend, Oregon. Augie was proud of his new bride and wanted the world to know. On their way home, they spent some time in Anchorage in search of an appropriate site for the transmitter for a new station, KENI radio.

Capt Lathrop had decided the time was right to locate a station in Anchorage. A couple of sites for the transmitter and tower were considered, but were ultimately rejected or denied. An appropriate transmitter/tower site was finally found at the mouth of Chester Creek. With the planning completed and an application approved, Augie moved to Anchorage as Midnight Sun technical director, to build the station in July of 1947. The KENI transmitter building was both beautiful and functional, and was situated in a wooded area overlooking Cook Inlet. It was a convenient ten-minute drive from downtown Anchorage. The antenna system contained the first co-axial line installation in the Territory. The KENI studios and offices were located in the new, million dollar Lathrop Building, which housed the Fourth Avenue Theater and the Lathrop Company offices. The studios were all equipped with the latest in acoustical and lighting technology. The theater itself was a masterpiece of design and beauty, and together with the new radio studios, provided a major tourist attraction in Anchorage. Capt Lathrop had done it again.

During this busy time, somewhere in the midst of KENI construction and moving between Anchorage and Fairbanks, Augie and Pat had their first child. A daughter, Robin Ann, was born on February 20, 1948.

On May 1, 1948, KENI radio went on the air. Al Bramstedt, Sr., then manager of KFAR, was sent down from Fairbanks. Augie remained chief engineer and technical director for Midnight Sun Broadcasting, as well as assuming management responsibilities at KFAR following Bram's transfer.

Augie wasn't a manager—he didn't want to be—but Capt asked him to try. When Capt needed someone to work out the bugs at the new station in the highly competitive Anchorage market, Bram moved back to Midnight Sun Headquarters in Fairbanks, and Augie relocated to Anchorage as manager of KENI radio. It was around Thanksgiving of 1949. Anchorage would be their home now. The house he and Pat bought had been built in 1916 as the residence of the military supervisor during the construction of the Alaska Railroad. It overlooked Cook Inlet, Sleeping Lady, and Mt. McKinley—an ideal location to appreciate the beauty of Alaska that Pat and Augie loved so much.

Early programming at KENI was patterned, for the most part, after the quality public service format of KFAR. "Mukluk Telegraph," an offspring of "Tundra Topics," provided a vital source for personal messages to the bush. Ruth Briggs, Augie's first hire as manager, produced her own women's radio program. The stations of Midnight Sun Broadcasting also had affiliation with both NBC and ABC, and received much of their programming on magnetic tape. A 'round-robin' circuit kept a quantity of tapes moving to and from Alaska with programs fresh from the networks. KENI was also affiliated with the Mutual Broadcasting System (MBS) for some services.

Live performances, both musical and theatrical, were produced in the KENI studios by Mary Hale, conductor of the Anchorage Community Chorus, and Frank Brink. The Chorus used Studio A at KENI for its rehearsal facilities in exchange for a Sunday afternoon concert once a month. The Chorus also performed special Easter and Christmas concerts for the station plus a thirty-minute program of great choral music each week.

The early 1950s saw the dawning of a new epoch in the history of broadcasting in Alaska. For Augie it was time filled with new beginnings—a new family, a new home, and a new professional standing. Augie was and always will be an engineer, but that foundation provided a disciplined approach in his management role. His engineering background was critical to his success in management and his foresight into the needs and technical potential of broadcasting in Alaska.

KFAR radio transmitter building and tower on Farmer's Loop Road, 1939.

Austin E. (Capt) Lathrop.

Downtown Fairbanks, 1939. KFAR studios in Lathrop Bldg. above *Daily News Miner*.

KFAR radio staff, 1940. Front Row (l. to r.): Mary Cash (recipes, etc.), Miriam Dickey (secretary/treasurer. KFAR), Jack Winston (manager. KFAR), Jean (steno, KFAR & Lathrop Co.). Back Row (l. to r.): Al Bramstedt (announcer), August Hiebert (engineer), George Meyers (newscaster), Jack Crawford (announcer), Bud Foster (announcer and assistant manager), Stan Bennett (chief engineer).

KFAR SPECIAL EDITION **KFAR**

Fairbanks Daily News-Miner

America's Farthest-North Daily Newspaper — Member of The Associated Press

VOLUME NO. XXVII • FAIRBANKS, ALASKA, SATURDAY, SEPTEMBER 30, 1939 • PRICE TEN CENTS

KFAR GIVES VOICE TO INTERIOR ALASKA

Chronicle of Alaska Traced in Footsteps Of KFAR President

Radio Brings World To Doorstep

ANGLE STUDY IN TOWERS

Most Modern Scientific Advances Incorporated In KFAR installations

Audience Is "Director" For Station

KFAR IGLOO AND TOTEM POLE

WHERE KFAR'S "WELCOME MAT" GREETS FAIRBANKS

Daily News Miner Special Edition newspaper article (Sept.ember 30, 1939) detailing Fairbank's first radio station, KFAR, operation and staff.

KFAR 'Battery' Of Engineers Rejoined As Team in Alaska

Stanton Bennett and August Hiebert Resume Work Together After Experience as Chief and Assistant Engineers in Radio Station at Bend, Ore.

"THIS MAKES IT TICK"

Radio Spurs Interest Of Music Lovers

HOW TO MAKE AN ENGINEER SMILE

Ex-Boy Scout Still Does Good Turns At Radio Dials, Knobs

Multitude Of Sportscasts Set for KFAR

W. E. 'Bud' Foster Will Retransmit Nation's Outstanding Athletic Events

CONSULTING ENGINEER CONSULTING

Seattle Firm Lauds Radio Venture Here

One Eye On Clock Needed For Foreign Reception

Radio "Windmill" Aids Reception In Isolated Areas

Photo by Augie Hiebert

A composite of 1940 Fairbanks transportation.

Sourdough Sunday Breakfast at Fowler's cabin, March 1940. Pictured left to right: Bud Foster, Stan Bennett, Mrs. Foster, Charlie Fowler, Patsy the Dog, Leonard Seppala, Mrs. Fowler, Sybil Godfrey (Miss Juneau), and Augie.

Day off for engineers! Stan Bennett on skis and Augie "driving" dog team.

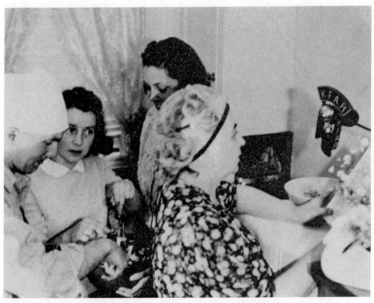

Mary Cash hosts radio program, "Kitchen Capers". Augie always came prepared for serious sampling.

Photo from Reud Griffen Collection, Accession Number SA-845-1073, in Archives. Alaska and Polar Regions Department, Univ.

Augie, engineer, and Al Bramstedt, announcer on "remote" broadcast at dog race checkpoint.

Facsimile Test Transmission
Fairbanks to New York
—Subject- KFAR Transmitter
Plant and QTH K7XSB
Sent Oct 5 1941

Facsimile test transmission sent from Fairbanks to New York.

Fax transmission sent from New York to Fairbanks, 1941.

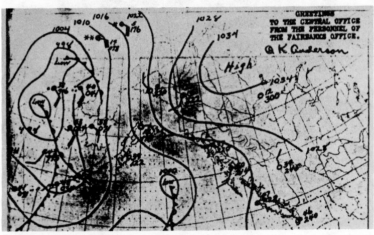

Facsimile test transmission of weather map. Was of convincing value for future Weather Bureau and military use of facsimile.

Caption Augie wrote to his mom with this picture: "A kid took this of me last spring when I drove Fowler's 'cat' to tow a house for Dr. Bramhall. He was putting in a magnetic observatory in connection with his Carnegie Institute work. Had a lot of fun."

Aftermath of Second Avenue, downtown Fairbanks fire,
at 60 degrees below zero.

Sparky and Charlie Fowler on trip with Augie to field test KFAR signal strength,
plus Stateside signals, in preparation for FCC clear channel case of July 1946
in Washington D.C.

In her eyes Sparky reflects the mirror image of her Master, as he too copied press. (Footnote: This is Pat Hiebert's favorite picture of Sparky. In her words, "Yes, this is what Augie looked like when he copied press.")

Ruben Gaines and Sparky singing Happy Birthday, KFAR, 1946.

Patricia Ann Stadler, second lieutenant, U.S. Army, 1946.

Pat and Augie Hiebert, March 16, 1947, at their wedding reception, Crescent Bar Community Hall.

KENI transmitter building, Anchorage, 1949.

CHAPTER 3

THROUGH THE MAGIC WINDOW: THE 1950s

E ven as a child, Augie Hiebert exhibited the classic symptoms of an over-achiever. He was driven by the excitement to accomplish, to do better, to tackle and solve a difficult task. The fear of failing or making a mistake drove him to do that much better, though the anxieties of disapproval or reprimand at times made him hesitant to approach the unfamiliar. Yet maturity begets self-assurance, and in his late twenties Augie observed in a letter to his mom and dad, "He who makes no mistakes, makes nothing at all. . . . Alaska, living here, working here with accompanying problems and experiences have contributed deeply to my mental development. I think it has done a job a lifetime somewhere else would have failed to do. And it's been of immeasurable value."

This realization and revelation capture the substance of the man who would be destined to mold the entire telecommunications future of Alaska.

Communications is the life-line to expand horizons and cultivate awareness in Alaska. To many people in areas remote and isolated, the broadcast media brings a sense of belonging . . . to their state, to their nation, to the rest of the world. Capt Lathrop was sensitive to this when he built KFAR in Fairbanks, and then KENI in Anchorage. He was a visionary, and his tragic death at his Healy River coal mine on

July 26, 1950, was a significant loss for Alaska.

But his spirit lives on . . . it lives within Augie Hiebert. Augie has been ahead of his time in broadcasting in Alaska. Without his impetus, follow through, and encouragement to others, many of the advancements in broadcasting in Alaska would not have been accomplished.

When Capt died, Midnight Sun Broadcasting changed. His business legacy survived, but the company's management priorities appeared to become more profit-oriented than people-oriented.

In 1949 there were 109 television stations in the lower forty-eight states. Television was beginning to emerge as a viable medium, though its profitability was yet to be realized. That year the FCC froze any further licensing due to a rapidly developing chaos in technical problems, interference, and coverage. To resolve the disorder, the FCC formulated an allocation plan and technical criteria—the same credo by which television lives today. In 1952 the freeze was lifted. Television appeared to be the wave of the future, and Midnight Sun sent Augie to New York to investigate the viability of television in Alaska.

The more he researched, the more Augie knew that television would be an answer to many of the people problems generated by isolation in Alaska. Augie recognized some of the consequences of a male-oriented social structure. Men had many opportunities for employment and other activities, such as hunting and fishing, but their families were often socially and culturally isolated. Some families chose not to stay; others experienced marital separation or breakup. Alaska's deficiencies were often criticized, and businesses had difficulty recruiting and hiring people. Television could help stabilize this unsatisfactory situation.

When Augie returned from his fact-finding trip, the

parent company to Midnight Sun, the Lathrop Company, which also owned the theater, decided the competition of television with the "big screen" would be counterproductive. The board of directors therefore rejected their original resolution to pursue television.

Augie was convinced and determined, though television was a risk in such a small market (54,000 people) with three radio stations, two newspapers, and two theaters. Despite all this, in July 1952 Northern Television, Inc., was formed. Strong loyalties to Midnight Sun motivated Augie to submit a proposal to establish the TV operation while still managing KENI radio, and then merge Northern Television with Midnight Sun. A merger concept was denied by the Lathrop Co. as well. The handwriting was on the wall. On July 25, 1953, Augie resigned from Midnight Sun Broadcasting to devote full efforts as president and general manager of his own company, Northern Television, Inc. Jack Walden, then chief engineer for Midnight Sun, had also tendered his resignation to become vice-president and technical director at Northern Television.

In the meantime, on May 18, 1953, an application had been filed with the FCC for the first television station in Alaska. On July 29, the final construction permit was issued for 3200-watt Channel 11 Anchorage. Equipment was ordered and by early September, a modest staff was recruited. The equipment arrived in mid-October and the process of installation began.

Blood, sweat, and probably some tears brought television to Alaska, but most of all a consuming love for Alaska, its people, and his work motivated Augie to beat the pavement in search of Alaskans to invest in his new company. Augie knew that if Capt Lathrop had been alive he would have invested in television for the very same reasons that he had built KFAR radio—to provide a service to the community.

Two major factors worked in Augie's favor to contribute to the success of television. First, the people in the community wanted it. Second, the business community recognized there were economic advantages with the advent of television.

A source of pride for Augie is that from the very beginning, Northern Television has been wholly Alaskan owned and operated. The two largest stockholders during the early years and the ones that were closest to him and gave him the most assistance were Wells Ervin and Max Kirkpatrick. Bob Baker, then vice-president of First National Bank of Anchorage, was also an early supporter and confidant. Twenty-five businessmen invested in NTV as original stockholders. They agonized over early losses, but they stuck with Augie through thick and thin—and continue to do so. In return Augie gives his total commitment to quality. With the stockholders' backing and the $25,000 seed money left to him by Capt Lathrop, Augie's dream, with its modest beginnings, was to be realized. One thing Augie learned from Capt was that if you start with quality, the foundation will be solid and will withstand the test of time.

Initially, two factors were the source of a great deal of frustration. One was the opposition to television by the Lathrop Company. The other was the application for a license by a California-based partnership, Kiggins and Rollins, one week after that filed by NTV. They not only filed for Channel 2 in Anchorage, but for Channel 2 in Fairbanks with call letters KFIA (First in Anchorage) and KFIF (First in Fairbanks). To survive and succeed in an already saturated advertising market became a more intensified challenge.

But these challenges were simply the first of many yet to come.

The first home of KTVA was the ground floor of the Mt. McKinley Building on Fourth and Denali. Offices and studio were based there, and the tower was atop the fourteen-floor apartment structure in downtown Anchorage.

Jack Walden, as technical director, supervised the equipment installation. In early October Jack was sent on a two-week fact finding trip to tour and inspect all new TV installations in the Pacific Northwest. Upon his return, installations commenced. He enlisted the help of local experts including Mike Peterson, an FAA electronics engineer, who was in charge of setting up the new Dumont transmitter. Dave Fulton, with Communication Equipment and Service Co., assisted with general wiring and equipment placement. Steel Fabricators, Inc. built the thirty-five-foot steel superstructure to support the thirty-seven-foot six Bay batwing antenna. The antenna and studio equipment were all GE and all state of the art. The GE package utilized was specifically designed for the smaller market operation for quality and functional efficiency. One person could run the operation from a single control point. It additionally permitted flexibility and adaptability for growth and expansion.

Jack Walden details some of the technical aspects of television transmission, with specific reference to the preference and choice of a channel. "Choosing channels is a technical problem in which factors of coverage, terrain, antenna height, power, and local conditions all contribute to make the proper choice for a given area extremely important." Even though three channels were available when NTV applied for their license in May 1953, Channel 11 was chosen. Walden elaborates as to the several reasons why Channel 11 was selected:

> First, it is in the VHF (very high frequency) band where man-made interference commercial shortwave transmitter harmonic and beat frequency interference as well as amateur radio

interference is at a minimum as compared to lower number channels. Alaskan cities are surrounded by a density of transmitting equipment probably not equalled in cities anywhere else in the world and this plus automobile ignition noise is less likely on the high band channels such as eleven.

Second, antenna elements, while accomplishing exactly the same functions, are smaller for both transmitting and receiving on channel eleven than on lower band channels, which means less cost to the viewer who may require an elaborate antenna system in the far outlying areas. Modern all-band receiving antennas, such as the fan and conical which are so popular now in Anchorage, are most efficient on or near channel eleven. And smaller elements mean less costly antenna installations on housetops—and smaller ones in an area where there is wind.

Third, the weight and size of the transmitting antenna itself is important from a safety and economic standpoint. Each set of 'batwings' or 'bays' adds to the efficiency or power 'gain' of the antenna system. In both Anchorage and Fairbanks, where channel eleven was the choice, six bays are used which gives an approximate effective power increase of approximately six, as compared to what one bay would produce alone that means additional clarity and coverage in outlying or suburban areas."

Many of the original staff at KTVA were part-time and

many came over from KENI radio. Frank Brink, Jack Dunhaver, Walt Welch, and Charles Connor had all previously worked for Midnight Sun, KENI radio. The full-time staff had specific responsibilities, but in most cases they soon became so diversified they could perform almost any task that needed to be done. To begin with, KTVA broadcast only four hours per day, signing on at 6:00 P.M. with one-half hour of test pattern (remember the Indian head?).

Northern Television was consumed not only in building, but in selling advertising for KTVA's start up date. The retail market was gearing up for Anchorage's first look at television. Television receivers sold like hot cakes!

KFIA received its construction permit from the FCC in late July, as did KTVA. Not wanting to commit very much money to the operation, KFIA used secondhand FM equipment. One FM transmitter was converted to an audio transmitter and another to a video transmitter. A homemade antenna was erected atop the Anchorage Westward Hotel Building; the business offices were located in the basement. Kiggins and Rollins claimed they would be first on the air on October 15, 1953.

KFIA went on the air the middle of October. The rebuilt transmitter didn't work, nor did the homemade antenna. People who had never seen television wondered, "So this is TV!?" Those who had seen television elsewhere thought, "So this is Alaskan TV!?" The knee-jerk response was that Alaskan's didn't know how to do anything. The sale of television advertising was adversely affected immediately, and retail TV sales, with inventories at their peak, plummeted. Retailers were frantic and wanted Augie to expedite his operation. Augie was patient; he knew he had to prove, now more than ever, that television would work. He had to sweeten the bitter taste left by the failed operations.

Augie was not about to let people down. So Jack

Walden and his crew worked diligently and quietly through the confusion. On Thanksgiving day, 1953, KTVA was ready for their test. The test picture was gorgeous! Augie even received a phone call from a man at Lake Minchumina: "Gee, we've got a nice picture over here." Augie said, "That's impossible; you're on the other side of the mountains." The man cordially offered to take a picture of the test pattern and send it to Augie. The photograph showed a terrific picture, the product of a phenomenon called knife edge refraction. The signal hit the top of Mt. McKinley and refracted over and focused down on Minchumina.

The chilling skepticism slowly, but surely, began to thaw. December 11 was chosen as the dedication date, to coincide with the channel number. The two week period from test to start would enable finalization of details, full completion of equipment hook up, and promotion of the official sign-on. On December 11, 1953, KTVA was the first official commercial television station in Alaska to go on the air.

The opening ceremonies were festive and demonstrated television's capabilities for community involvement and public affairs presentations (see the Appendix for the text of this opening ceremony). Amidst the pomp and circumstance, Anchorage also celebrated its fellowship with the military community. (The civilian and military interface in Anchorage has long contributed to a stable society.) Along with live military choral and band arrangements were local dance and vocal talents. The first sponsors of regular programs on KTVA were applauded for their pioneering support and faith in television as a new and Alaska-owned industry. Staff members were introduced and described their professional contributions to the operation.

The thirty-minute ceremonies were to be followed by the regularly scheduled programming. But since the film for "Range Riders" with Jack Malone did not arrive, it was replaced by "March of Time through the Ages," a discussion of the underlying criminal element in your town. Not only did Augie lose his first scheduled program, he almost lost his first sponsor, Sunrise Bakery.

During the first two years of operation, KTVA was affiliated with the NBC and Dumont networks. Initially, it was difficult to get network programs to Alaska. The sponsors who bought advertising in network programming had to ask for Alaska and had to pay for Alaska. This was not only costly, but many of the advertisers simply were not interested in Alaska because the population was so small. Procter & Gamble was a major exception. Jim Lanham, their sales representative based in Alaska, had set pioneering precedents in sponsorship of Alaskan radio. Seeing the virtues of television, he applied his company's advertising dollars to program sponsorship. The only alternative to network programming for NTV was syndicated shows, which were expensive—almost exceeding potential revenues the first year of operation. "Canned" programs were on sixteen-millimeter film; they were bulky, heavy, and costly to ship compared to the contemporary taped versions. Later, the network changed its policy to a blanket disposition of programming. Programs were automatically sent, rather than having to be ordered by the network clients. Northern TV would be paid for whatever advertising spots were in a program. (See the Appendix for KTVA's program schedule for the first week of television in Alaska.)

Many of the early programs were local shows, produced live in the KTVA studios. These shows fulfilled a twofold purpose: they filled in where network programming was deficient, and they filled a need in the community for public information. A talented staff originated a great deal of the local programs. A few of the shows involved live studio audience participation, while others embraced the realm of community activities. These included, "Your Army Neighbor," "Ford Richardson in Review," "University of Alaska— Extension Service," Fred Thomas's "What's Going On" and the quiz show "Pan for Gold," Tex Noey's "Know Alaska," Norma Goodman's "Hostess House," Paul West's "Buckaroo Club" for children, Frank Feeman's "Hi Jinx," Hal Knudsen's "Hal's Pals" (he also surfaced as Sourdough Dan the Weatherman), and Ethel Oliver's "Through the Magic Window."

With live television you live and learn. In retrospect even the most catastrophic "out-takes" were funny. At least there was no video tape to make a permanent record. Local advertising was also produced live, leaving its own memorable mark.

Norma Goodman's debut in commercials, January 1954, was as spokesperson for Piggly Wiggly, advertising a new product—frozen meat pies. One of her more famous live commercials was a demonstration of a canned milk product, reportedly as good as the real thing. Her response to a large gulp of the flavorful liquid was, "Mmmmm." Then her microphone was supposed to have been cut as the commercial went to a slide with a voice over. Her microphone, however, was still on when all who were tuned in heard her say, "Yuck!" The milk she had tasted was sour.

Fred Thomas, a normally poised public affairs interviewer, was on occasion "up-staged" by his guests. Once when the circus was in town, Fred interviewed a performer who had brought with him a boa constrictor in a burlap bag. Under the hot studio lights, the snake eventually emerged from the bag, wound itself around Fred's leg, and stuck its head above the table. Fred ended that interview—and show—quickly!

Then there was Dagmar, the scantily clad night club performer, who visited Anchorage and appeared on Fred's show. Dagmar did most of the talking that night, vivid in every way, and reduced Fred to blush and stammer. At the end of the show she captured the true magic of "color" on a black and white screen. As Dagmar waved to the camera, she quickly turned and thoroughly bussed her unexpected host.

• • •

By now Augie's reputation for civic leadership was well established, and he took those responsibilities seriously. At the time KTVA was receiving final construction modification, Augie was president of the Anchorage Chamber of Commerce and active in the Civil Air Patrol as commanding officer of the Anchorage Communications Squadron. When the Alaskan Command Civilian Advisory Board was formed in the early 1950s, Augie was appointed to membership. The Board was a liaison between the community and the military to foster friendly communication and promote a good working relationship subsequent to the war. Augie's recognition of the value of the military—its resources (economic, social, and cultural) and impact on a community—is rooted in his war-time experiences in Fairbanks.

Over many changes in Command during which the Advisory Board was disbanded and reappointed, Augie remained a member. The activity of the civilian board was dependent on the leadership of the Command, internal leadership of the board itself, and of course the necessity for intensified liaison.

As a communications officer with the Civil Air Patrol, Augie helped build a communications site, as well as train cadets. Although dedication to his personal business superseded a long active duty with the CAP, his later involvement in the early 1960s as an honorary member would have a monumental consequence on the quality of life on the "last frontier."

Two events during Augie's term as Chamber of Commerce president merit mention. He successfully pushed for the use of $72,000 in Chamber funds to rebuild the Sidney Lawrence Auditorium, which had burned down. He also spearheaded the Chamber's support of Anchorage's fight to obtain port authority and dock facilities. Augie's public statement as Chamber president reflected that resolve: "We are of the definite opinion that justification and feasibility of a port in Anchorage have been proven. . . . There is more economic justification for a port here than in any other city in Alaska. We no longer want to take a back seat. If we have to, we will send people to Washington, D.C. and spare no effort to assure a port in Anchorage."

During the early 1950s, Augie was also an active ham radio operator and a leader in a civil defense contingency for the Anchorage area, which involved a network of amateur radio operators. By authority of the FCC, the Radio Amateur Civil Emergency Services (RACES) was established. Augie assumed direction of Anchorage's emergency communication's council, established in 1951 as a stepped-up effort to form a communication control center in the event of an emergency in Anchorage. Augie's job was to coordinate the emergency stations involving amateur radio operators, Civil Air Patrol operators, and the municipal radio system.

While Augie nurtured his dreams, Pat gave birth to and raised three more daughters: Mary Margaret (July 14, 1950), Catherine Josephine (November 3, 1954), and Theresa Lucy (August 17, 1958). Pat took seriously her daughters' growing up in the public eye. Her constant admonition was, "Girls, wherever you go, you represent the Hiebert family." The meaning was clear, and the daughters responded with pride.

Anchorage now had television, and soon Fairbanks wanted it. But to put television in Fairbanks would be an even more difficult challenge—the population was much smaller, less than half the size of Anchorage. The people in Fairbanks knew Augie and they knew of his operation in Anchorage, and so they approached him to start television in Fairbanks. Even though Kiggins and Rollins had applied for a station in Fairbanks, Channel 2, construction permits had not been activated. The Lathrop Company remained steadfast in its opposition to television; they had no intention of starting a station in Fairbanks.

In August of 1954, only a few months after the dedication of KTVA in Anchorage, Wells Ervin and Augie drove to Fairbanks to meet with local businessmen who had expressed interest in stock investment. The support was enough to get started. On September 1, Augie announced plans to build KTVF-TV in Fairbanks. That announcement, distilled from a local news report, reflects Augie's policy, principles, and dedication to serve the public:

> It has been our opinion that the key to successful television operation in Alaska is when ownership is retained by the businessmen and investors of the city which the station is to serve. This philosophy of ownership has been extremely successful in Anchorage and will be equally so in Fairbanks.
>
> The Fairbanks TV Station will be built with brand new factory General Electric equipment, patterned after the installation of KTVA in Anchorage. This equipment is the latest and best money can buy, and produces a picture which is the highest quality obtainable. We intend to file for the same channel KTVA uses, Channel 11, due to the

excellent experience we have had through operation there. The equipment is economical to install and operate, requires only small and lightweight elements on homes which may need outside antennas, and is ideal to serve this particular area. We find that Channel 11 is entirely free of interference such as is quite frequently experienced on lower channels by ignition noise, amateur radio operation, and commercial shortwave transmitters which are so common near Alaskan cities.

We have found that television becomes a part of the Alaskan home and is greatly appreciated. It provides entertainment, news, education, religion, civic and community activities, all brought into the home and enjoyed by young and old alike. The entire family is entertained by television, and of course it is especially appreciated by shut-ins or those who have difficulty in participating in various forms of outside entertainment. The residents of Fairbanks and vicinity, as well as the military personnel at Ladd and Eielson Air Force Bases owe a debt of gratitude to the spirit of the Fairbanks businessmen who are going to make this installation possible. Completion of the present plan of installation will mean that top TV programming will be seen in Fairbanks early in 1955.

We at KTVA have felt for some time that Fairbanks deserved to have a television station, and would support it as enthusiastically as Anchorage has supported ours. However, we felt that before approaching Fairbanks investors with a plan we should gain enough experience and knowledge of the industry as can be applied to Alaskan cities, to assure success of such an undertaking. Our primary interest in presenting this plan to Fairbanks is to assure the best possible television service to this city, technically and from a programming and advertising stand-point, so that the operation is one which will reflect community pride and participation. By having an operational arrangement between the local TV stations of both cities, programming costs for each will be greatly reduced, increased advertising revenue from national manufacturers can be realized, which in turn results in superior programming and a more successful operation.

Formation of a Television Company adds another important industry to rapidly growing and expanding Fairbanks. It means a new payroll and more advertising dollars entering Alaska from the States, both of which adds to the economy of the city. It also offers a new means of expression to aid in the development of the area economically, as well as through civic and cultural functions.

The wheels were put in motion, an FCC license was applied for, and the equipment was ordered.

Meanwhile, KFIA-TV in Anchorage was in financial ill health, and had been from the beginning. Poor equipment was to blame for much of the difficulty, but by August 1953

Kiggins and Rollins were on the verge of going broke. By early October 1954, Kiggins had pulled out of the partnership, and Rollins agreed to sell to Midnight Sun. Transfer of ownership included the disposition of the construction permit for KFIF-TV, Channel 2, in Fairbanks. Midnight Sun immediately issued a press release that they would be first on the air in Fairbanks. And the race that wasn't meant to be was on.

Not only was the energy of the race documented in newspaper releases, but it remains vividly imprinted in the minds of the people who were there. The Lathrop Company, with its ownership of the *Fairbanks Daily News-Miner*, provided the majority of the publicity. Augie mostly worked again in patience and silence.

Television in Fairbanks was more of an emotional issue than in Anchorage. There are probably several reasons. For one, Fairbanks was literally the end of the road; it was the last outlet of metropolitan U.S.A. People there are independent and resourceful and do things with a passion. They felt the isolation from family and friends outside. They knew they would have to work harder for television to survive. The market was barely large enough for one television station, much less two. The anxiety was probably predictable. But one thing people in Alaska do well is rally to an occasion, no matter what the odds. And in Alaska the stakes are usually incredibly high.

A thread runs through the story of Augie Hiebert—he is a man ahead of his time. That's the bottom line. But the fine print is the love, respect, and trust that people share for him. People were disposed to feel, "If you're selling, we'll buy." That has been a foundation for growth in telecommunications for Alaska.

On November 4, 1954, two pioneer broadcast firms joined forces to provide better programming for Alaska radio and television audiences. The affiliation was consummated to also provide many sales advantages to local and national advertisers. William J. (Bill) Wagner, president of Alaska Broadcasting System, Inc. and owner of Alaska Broadcast Company, organized Alaska's first broadcasting system. His company was responsible for the acquisition or construction of six CBS affiliated radio stations throughout the state, including KFQD radio in Anchorage, KFRB in Fairbanks, and stations in Juneau, Ketchikan, Sitka, and Seward.

The merger also meant the affiliation of Northern Television with the CBS network on July 23, 1955. Augie's prior affiliation with NBC had been somewhat frustrating because it was a big network and not responsive to the smaller affiliates. Their compensation rate was low and they were often slow to reply to correspondence. The affiliation with CBS has afforded Augie the unique opportunity to maintain, even as a small market operation, a close working relationship with those at the executive level.

KTVF, Channel 11, the first commercial television station to officially go on the air in Fairbanks, held its dedicatory ceremonies the evening of February 17, 1955, having beaten KFAR-TV by nearly two weeks. KTVF facilities were centrally located in the Northward Building with transmitter, offices, and studio in the basement and the tower on top. KTVF's dedication was as festive as that of its sister station in Anchorage only fourteen months prior. It was an encore performance in every way. Fairbanks dignitaries, local talent, and the military joined the public in the live program. Those who either had no TV or wished to avoid the crowded Northward lobby congregated around store windows where television receivers had been installed for the occasion.

Many Anchorage residents, business people, and KTVA representatives shared in the celebration, courtesy of a charter flight provided by Alaska Airlines. An official motorcade brought guests from the airport to downtown Fairbanks for the festivities. It was a gala event in keeping with its historic significance.

KTVF was dedicated to the same public service principles upon which Northern Television based its operation in Anchorage. The staff was small and included a couple of KTVA transfers, such as station manager Walt Welch. Programming reflected a cross-section of much of the community with locally produced children's, military, educational, and sports shows.

Augie was now thirty-eight years old. He had successfully helped build two radio stations, KBND and KFAR; had designed and built a radio station, KENI; founded his own company, Northern Television Inc.; and built two television stations, KTVA and KTVF. Four days after KTVF went on the air, Augie was elected to honorary membership in Fairbanks Pioneer Igloo No. 4 for his pioneering efforts in radio and television in Alaska. On April 4, 1955, he was initiated into the prestigious fraternity. Members of this organization must be native-born Alaskans or have lived in the state thirty years. Augie had been in Alaska only sixteen years. The Pioneer organization has awarded very few memberships with full entitlement. Others who have been so honored include President Warren G. Harding; Col. Carl Ben Eielson and Joe Crosson, pioneer aviators; and Wiley Post and Will Rogers.

When KTVA celebrated its second anniversary on December 11, 1955, Augie credited the station's success to the commitment of local investors and to loyal advertisers and viewers:

> It seems very appropriate that our anniversary
> here at KTVA comes between Thanksgiving
> and the first of a New Year. For we feel not

only very grateful for all we've received in the past, but are looking ahead toward being able to give more and more in return in the years to come.

There were two years ago a score or more of sincere and highminded men who decided to take a chance on Alaska Television, and while many of them were far from sure they'd even get their investment back, they were certain they were doing a good thing to bring a new medium to this new land. They know now that their investments worked out.

Two years ago a hundred more businessmen paid hard-earned money for advertising at a rate high enough to allow television to operate here in its early days as a gesture of support as much as any hope of business return. These businessmen now reach an expanded market and are receiving their full value with more to come.

There were two years ago, and are now, a steadily growing group of thousands and thousands of television viewers who at first didn't get all they wanted perhaps, in the way of entertainment and information from the news medium. Now, with top rated CBS and our local programming all the time, we are sure we will be able to offer more and more of what television really ought to be.

It's been at times difficult, but certainly a good two years for us at Northern Television. For we know we have, with the support of all of you, built something we'll continue to build.

Augie's efforts to develop and mold a well-balanced environment for those who called Anchorage and Alaska home reflects his commitment to public service through television. Art and music were aspects of life that were integral to the health and growth of a community, especially one so isolated. Dr. George and Mary Hale vividly capture Augie's involvement:

> Augie Hiebert's contributions to the arts in Anchorage and the State of Alaska have been so numerous that we've lost count— hundreds of hours of his own time have been invested in fund-raising, long-range planning and advising the Anchorage Community Chorus, the Alaska Festival of Music, the Anchorage Community Theatre, and the Alaska Council on the Arts. And he has been a staunch advocate of the arts in business circles, with politicians and with our elected officials—no person has been a more effective supporter of the arts than Augie.

The Festival of Music, held every June from 1956 through 1966, was all consuming for the community as Alaskans, young and old, feasted on concerts, lectures, and workshops in music, art, and dance. KTVA offered a cost-free educational series of festival lectures. It was a time alive with formal and informal congregations of Alaskans and guest performers from the Lower 48. The project was successfully organized on a shoestring and involved a platoon of volunteers. Many homes in the community opened their doors to guest artists. It was exciting to have the opportunity to meet celebrity participants such as Julius Herford, conductor Robert Shaw, pianist John Wustman (now personal accompanist to Pavoratti), and so many others.

Northern TV acquired its own national representative office in Seattle in 1957. Bill Wagner, who was vice-president of national sales for Northern TV, having associated in 1954, had sold his six radio stations and was advised for medical reasons to divest of his remaining business, the office in Seattle. Alaska Radio and TV Sales, therefore, became part of the Northern TV family and remained a valuable asset to the flow of national sales for almost thirty years.

Disaster struck the Fairbanks television operation on a Sunday in January 1957. A fire in the Northward Building was thought to have destroyed the station. Engineers Jack Walden and Chuck Peterson worked at a fevered pitch to repair smoke and water damage. A fifty foot section of the transmission line suffered direct fire damage. Within a few days the station was back on the air, but not before KFAR-TV graciously permitted the airing of two Sunday programs for crippled KTVF! In a disaster even competitors rally to the other's needs.

The 1950s saw the Korean War, the Cold War, Khrushchev, Sputnik, and Radio Free Europe (RFE). In the mid-1950s Bill Burke, an advertising executive in Seattle and Pacific Northwest regional manager for Radio Free Europe, asked Augie to manage Radio Free Europe in Alaska. Administration of the program mostly involved organizing annual fund-raising projects. In those days fund-raising campaigns were coordinated to support federal projects. In 1959 a DC-7 was chartered to fly RFE people from New York to tour RFE facilities in Europe. The transmitters were in Portugal, near Lisbon, and the studio and officers in Munich, Germany. For Augie, the excursion into Germany, the home of his ancestors, was memorable.

In the late 1950s and throughout the next decade,

Augie was involved in several extracurricular programs for high school age youth. These programs promoted self-respect, self-confidence, responsibility, dependability, creativity, and constructive and enduring resolution. Many young people were active in Radio Free Europe and participated in the fund-raising projects. Augie also took interest in Anchorage Science Fairs and served for a time as director of the program. Augie followed the progress of many young prospective engineers who had successfully designed and built highly technical projects.

In 1958 a live television program produced and directed entirely by young people, for young people, debuted on KTVA. "The Varsity Show," a local version of "American Bandstand," ran once a week for fourteen years. One-fourth of the proceeds from the show went into a college scholarship fund, which was divided equally among the crew.

The late 1950s were also filled with expansion and diversification. It was a period of more firsts for the already established pioneer broadcaster.

Muzak was the initial diversification endeavor, although FM radio was in the developmental stages of realization at the time. Anchorage didn't have Muzak and Augie knew it was popular elsewhere. Everywhere he went there was Muzak. Augie contacted the main office to explore the possibilities of obtaining a franchise and found out that two other outfits had similarly inquired. One of the competitors was big, ITT, who had the service contract for maintaining the Dew Line installations built in the mid-1950s.

A Muzak vice-president was sent to evaluate the qualifications of the applicants for the franchise. Northern TV was awarded the franchise and commenced its subscribed music service in 1959. Initial transmission was over telephone lines. The phone company at the time was less than cooperative, downright resistant, and excessively expensive. The operation over phone lines, even so, persisted for several years until it was found to be cheaper to use an FM subcarrier to transmit. It was not only cheaper, but this method provided better quality.

In their carpool from Fairbanks to Anchorage in September 1959, Mary Hale spoke to Augie and Jack Walden of the need in Anchorage for a source of good classical music. This was prior to subsidized public radio, and would therefore require paid advertising. They talked of audience, viable sources for financial support, and about FM stations on the East Coast that had made a go of it. As Mary puts it, "Augie sent for programs and information and he and Jack had many a discussion, I'm sure, about how in a market with very few FM sets this sort of broadcast service could be feasible, or even possible."

Finally, after much contemplation and frequent pencil sharpening, Northern Television decided to launch Alaska's first FM station. It was a major undertaking and a hard-sell because of the few sets in town. Augie knew, however, that FM offered a high quality signal and that it would eventually establish a market niche among the growing culturally aware and hungry population.

On September 15, 1960, KTVA-FM went on the air as the first FM station in Alaska. Those who had an FM set heard very few ads; to say it was noncommercial was true, but not by design. It was difficult to promote FM when there were no receivers. A couple of things were done to stimulate interest. One was offering automobile manufacturers special advertising rates to promote FM reception in their cars. Another was a monthly FM program guide sent to those who requested it.

Peter Herford, son of Julius Herford, associated with the Festival of Music, was news director for KTVA-TV. His family background in classical music lent well to his management of the first FM station with its classical music format. Peter had come to Alaska with his dad for the Festival. After completing his undergraduate studies at Columbia University, he wanted to come back to Alaska, but he needed a job. Peter wrote the cleverest application Augie had ever seen; he was bright and energetic. He started at the station as an announcer, then became news director along with assuming the duties of managing the FM station. Later, Peter won a CBS News Fellowship for extended studies at Columbia University, then climbed the CBS News ladder from the Cronkite news department to a producer of "60 Minutes" to vice-president of CBS News Affiliate Services.

Marv Weatherly, a technical engineer with KTVA-TV, was KTVA-FM's first announcer. Marv will be acknowledged many times to come as an alumnus of the telecommunications fraternity.

On August 5, 1961, KTVA-FM became the more recognizable KNIK-FM. There had been an understandable confusion with the use of the same call letters for TV and radio. The KNIK call letters were originally a ship's identification. When the ship was retired and the call letters became available, with FCC approval, KNIK was adopted. KNIK was chosen in honor of Knik, the first town founded on Cook Inlet.

KNIK-FM was the first FM station in the country to carry the Texaco Opera, by virtue of Augie's undying persistence. It took four to five years of talks with Texaco for Augie to convince them of the enhanced quality of FM stereo. They finally bought it. Texaco had previously broadcast their opera programming over high power AM stations; it had been a tradition for many years. Now, more FM than AM stations throughout the country subscribe to the ever popular Texaco Opera.

Augie has been a constant crusader for the right of people throughout Alaska to have access to communications, which led to another of his early Alaska pioneering adventures—translators. The history of translators reflects the appetite of people in remote areas, especially in the Rocky Mountains, for access to television.

Television is line-of-site. If an obstacle, such as a mountain, is between you and the signal, you get no reception. In the late 1950s those who wanted TV in remote areas weren't much daunted by these limitations or the fact that it is illegal to transmit without an FCC license. One of the first methods used was the repeater, a receiver and a receiving antenna placed on the top of a mountain. A mini-transmitter then transmitted the signal down to the area to be serviced. The problem was that the receiving antenna had to be on one side of the mountain and the transmitter on the other to avoid video feedback and internal interference from the operation itself.

An improvement on this idea was to translate the transmitter frequencies to another channel. If Channel 11, say, could be picked up and converted to Channel 4 by a translator, they not only wouldn't interfere with each other, but interference with the receiving signal would be eliminated. A directional antenna was used to transmit a signal successfully over considerable distance with exceptional quality.

The FCC had no rules or regulations for this rapidly growing concern, which at its peak served some 500,000 people in the Rocky Mountain region alone. Realizing that they could not put 500,000 people in jail, the FCC responded with rules to regulate the use of translators.

Augie had heard about translators; they seemed a natural solution for providing television reception in remote areas. Translators were worth testing in Alaska.

In the summer of 1958, prior to the legalization of translators, Augie invited an engineer from South Dakota to bring one of his cottage industry-built translators to Alaska. The location Augie chose for a test—at Suntrana south of the Fairbanks station—offered the worst possible conditions. Augie wanted to try the translator in Suntrana because that was where in the early days Capt had wanted his radio signal from Fairbanks to be received. Suntrana is a very isolated community of about 250 people. It is located about 125 miles from Fairbanks, in a valley marked by a 2,500-foot ridge. Capt even sent Augie to find out (in Capt's words) "why in the so and so doesn't my so and so radio station get into my so and so coal village." The problem was more than Capt could handle.

On that summer Sunday, Jack Walden and Augie, along with several mining company volunteers, rendezvoused for the translator test. Their two-way radio, a civil defense model, was tube operated (no transistors) and required a large and heavy storage battery for its power source. These, as well as an invertor and the antennas (receiving and transmitting), were carried up the 2,500-foot hill. Jack remained at the base station in a small house to monitor the test on his TV receiver. It took Augie two to three hours to make a trail to the top. ("I was so tired, I had to lift my feet up by my pant legs to climb up there.") The weight of the equipment packs was consuming. To lighten the load, they concluded that tree limbs could serve for the antenna poles. However, once they reached the top, they realized there were no trees. They were above timberline! Unsure whether hand held antennas would work, they finally found two gnarled branches to use as poles, one for the receiving antenna pointed to Fairbanks and one for the transmitting antenna pointed toward Jack at the base station.

There was an anxious moment when they made

contact with Jack. Was there a signal or not? Jack replied slowly, "Augie, I know that was a tough climb and you probably wonder, 'Was it all worth it,' but you oughta see what I've got down here." Word of the test had made its way to Suntrana. Jack described a small room filled with at least thirty kids all lying on the floor waiting for the "magic window" to come alive. The test proved positive, and just in time for Lassie! The kids were glued to the TV. Jack relayed the unfolding drama to the top, and Lassie was allowed to be seen in its entirety.

The following spring the FCC authorized the use of translators, and in 1959 Northern Television installed at Suntrana the first permanent translator in Alaska.

Permanent, yes; moose and wind proof, no! To supply power to the tube-operated equipment on top of the ridge, exceptionally durable wire was used. When the engineers ran the wire to the top and hooked the powerline to it, they found a significant voltage drop. They needed 115 volts to operate the system; but 115 on the bottom meant only 60 on top. So a 225 voltage system was used on the bottom to supply the needed 115 volts on top. Shortly thereafter, an antenna splitter was installed to feed some of the signal to the Usibelli Mine to the left and Healy to the right. Everyone in the valley then had television.

Winds are notoriously strong in the Healy-Suntrana area, especially along that ridge. So it was tough keeping TV on the air there. Once when it went off the air, the wires were found scattered all over the countryside. A moose had tangled itself in the maze. This was not a unique incident. Another time a moose tangled with shack and antennas, knocking the whole operation half way down the hill. That first facility remains in operation, at increased power, with antennas and buildings guy-wired and tied securely down!

• • •

The campaign for Alaska's admission to the Union had begun as early as 1915. Finally, on July 7, 1958, President Dwight D. Eisenhower signed the Statehood Bill, and on January 3, 1959, Alaska became the forty-ninth state, Many dedicated people had worked for Alaska's statehood for many years. It was an emotional time.

Hoisting antenna for first commercial television station in Alaska, KTVA, Channel 11, atop fourteen-story McKinley Building., Anchorage, 1953.

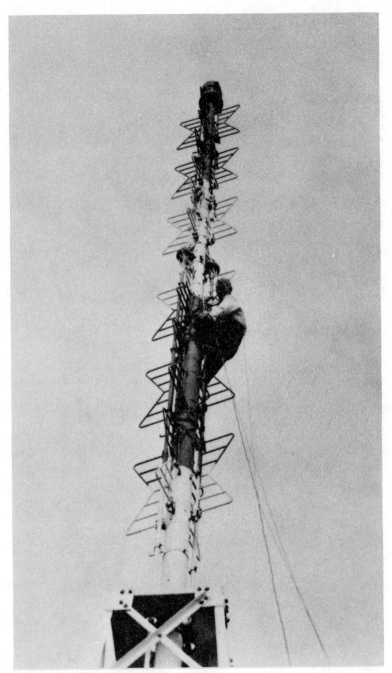

Augie inspecting new TV antenna.

Augie's view of Anchorage from tower vantage, looking toward Cook Inlet.
Note low profile of Anchorage skyline in 1953.

Fred Thomas and Norma Goodman in setting of live television commercial,
KTVA studio, in mid-1950s.

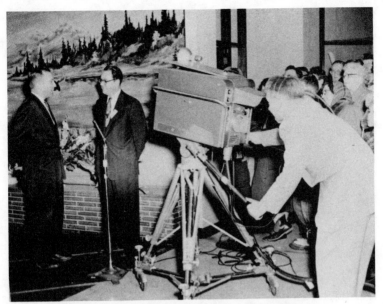

Opening ceremonies, KTVF-TV, Fairbanks, February 17, 1955.
Pictured from left: Al Bramstedt, Walt Welch (station manager, KTVF),
and Augie filling in on live camera.

KTVF dignitaries in caravan departing Fairbanks airport for
station opening at downtown Northward Building.

Suntrana first translator test in Alaska, 1959.

CHAPTER 4

STORMY WEATHER: THE 1960s

T he 1960s were filled with bittersweet memories of Mother Nature. She could bend and twist and inundate man's earthly fashionings, but she could not budge the steel will within Augie Hiebert.

In spite of the tumultuous loss, the decade was a time of conception, birth, and growth. The Alaska Broadcasters Association was created, satellite communication for Alaska was realized, and the foundations for state telecommunications policy were laid.

In 1960 Augie purchased his first tuxedo. The occasion for the formal attire was Augie's presentation to Norma Goodman of the prestigious Gold Mike Award, presented to the broadcaster performing in 1960 the greatest service to the community. Norma's show, "Hostess House," made its debut on March 5, 1954, shortly after KTVA began operations. Norma used "Hostess House" to seek solutions to the problems of people taking up a new life in the unique environment of Alaska. The recognition was well-merited. Known as the "First Lady of Television," Norma has continued for over three decades to serve the public interest.

As a broadcaster, Augie has remained vigilant in the promotion of quality programming. Sensitive to the educational opportunities that the electronic media can provide, Augie has been a benefactor for young people in Alaska.

In the fall of 1960, Augie participated in a panel discussion on the effects of television on the learning of young children. Carolyn Guess, a bright young teacher from Lake Otis Elementary School, was also a panel participant, and she and Augie engaged in some good-natured sparring. Their interaction on the panel helped establish one of the greatest mutual admiration societies of all time. Their paths have crossed in educational broadcasting many times and in many ways over the years.

When they met again in 1962, Carolyn was Miss Carolyn, the first "Romper Room" lady for the first nationally syndicated television show in Alaska. "Romper Room," the predecessor to popular educational shows such as "Sesame Street," was dedicated to learning, listening, and participating activities for preschool children. Kindergarten was not a part of the local public school curriculum at the time, so "Romper Room" was an important instructional tool, teaching young children the alphabet and basic number skills. Each week six children were on the program live, and no doubt the many who participated remember the smiling DO-BEE and the grouchy DON'T-BEE, the basket song, and the Magic Mirror.

There are many aspects of education in Alaskan broadcasting in which Augie has had an interest and influence. He has served as mentor to many young people who entered the business and matured under his wing. Augie's interest is linked to his own beginnings in broadcasting, in which he was given the opportunity and latitude to develop a unique identity. His guidance, inspiration, and motivation can bring out latent abilities in others.

All of Augie's survival resources and instincts were called upon to endure Alaska's Good Friday earthquake on March 27, 1964. In Anchorage the intensity was severe, the extent of damage ranging from absolute to minor. No one, however, was immune from the physical, emotional, or economic impact.

Augie was in his small office in the northeast corner of the ground floor of the McKinley Building. He was on the phone talking to Mike Peterson of Yukon Radio Supply. The phone went dead and the building started to rattle. It kept rattling and shaking, sending to the floor anything not adequately secured. What flashed through Augie's mind were questions about Northern Television's very survival:

> I was pretty sure from the action of the building that the tower had broken off. And the thought crossed my mind that if the antenna is broken and gone, plus whatever other damage has been done, it is probably the end of Northern TV. If it's still up there, there's still hope—one of those symbolic things that cross your mind. That antenna was what was flashing before my eyes, and I ran out the door when everything quieted down and looked up—and there it was! I thought, by George, we're gonna make it.

The next day Augie climbed the antenna to take a closer look. One lead wire was broken, which he soldered. Up close it was not discernible, but from a distance he could see that one of the supporting pipes was tilted slightly. There was a wrinkle in it—bent, but not broken. It would be a constant reminder of that Good Friday, from then through the move to a new location.

Building damage was extensive; it was in a shambles. Above Augie's office was a hole in the concrete the size of a nineteen-inch TV screen. The exposed iron reinforcement bar, the size of a man's wrist, was broken. The water pipes had broken and all power was lost. Rubble was scattered throughout. The fourteen-story structure, however, maintained its integrity because the stairwell and elevator shaft, the core of the building, held together. Cracks in the concrete were later patched and broken windows replaced.

An initial evaluation of damage to the station itself was pretty grim; however, except for water damage to the transmitter and some other equipment, the only item lost was a tube that had rolled off a maintenance bench.

The station was cold and dark and wet. When power was finally restored, the task to clean up and dry out began. Certain innovations had to be employed to endure mostly the cold. Cold running water was restored by tapping the main line in the basement. In order to heat the first floor during the next two winters, oil stoves were fired up in each office with stove pipes vented out the windows. This arrangement worked well, until the first north wind blew soot back into the rooms and killed the fires. Subsequently, a collector arrangement was set up incorporating all the pipes into one which extended up to a second floor window, through the second floor hallway and into the incinerator shaft which vented through a chimney the height of the building.

Between live programs the studio was filled with the racket and warmth of a space heater. Studio lights helped maintain a toasty atmosphere during live shows, such as "Hostess House" and "Romper Room," which Miss Carolyn ran alone; the building remained a "hard hat" area and children were understandably not permitted in the studio. For two years Northern Television would remain the only tenant in the tomb-like building.

The immediate post-earthquake period was difficult. Business was slow for both the television and FM stations. Loss of merchandise and uncertainty about federal disaster relief to businesses in the community influenced NTV sales accounts. It was a depressing and confusing time for many people. The light at the end of the tunnel was the prospect of reconstruction with a predicted "post-war" type boom.

The most difficult part of the earthquake's aftermath for NTV was the necessity to relocate. The operation could not remain in the McKinley Building. Although the move was expensive, many good things came of it. Building something new was a morale booster for Augie; building is in his blood.

At the same time, KBYR in Anchorage and KFRB in Fairbanks were being run by Chet Gordon, who had lost his manager and was trying to conduct the operation by himself. The timing was right for a business opportunity of mutual benefit. Augie checked with the FAA to verify the suitability of property in Spenard, a suburb to the south of Anchorage about three or four miles. This was a less expensive site than the original Anchorage townsite, where scarcity of land was driving up land and building prices. There was no problem; a 392-foot tower could be raised on the two-acre parcel in the middle of Spenard. Negotiations began for the transfer of the Gordon properties, and the sale was completed eight to nine months later. Application was made with the FCC for moving KTVA and KNIK to the new location as well as transfer of KBYR and KFRB to Northern Television, Inc. All transfers were finalized in August 1965.

The financial burden for this event was not too bad. With the support of Dan Cuddy of First National Bank of Anchorage, a Small Business Administration (SBA) low-interest loan was granted for construction of a building on the newly acquired land. In anticipation of constructing this new facility, Augie made a tour of Anchorage to see what types of structures withstood the earthquake. One type of building remained consistent in its structural stability, the

Butler building. When Augie saw that no damage had been done to Butler structures, he was convinced that was the structure he wanted for his facility. Not only was the Butler building stable, but its designs were aesthetically pleasing.

Construction began on the 7,200-square-foot building shortly after the August 1965 transfers were finalized. Rebuilding took time, but the Broadcast Center in its present location and form was dedicated in November 1966. It was now the home of KTVA-TV, KNIK-FM, KBYR-AM, and Muzak. It was a big day for Northern Television, Inc.

The modern, new facilities contained new equipment to avail an overnight move with no loss of air time. The rebuilt transmitter, ten times more powerful, coupled with a higher antenna afforded an expanded broadcast coverage area.

But when it rains, it pours. And so it did on August 15, 1967, in Fairbanks. The Chena River crested through downtown Fairbanks, destroying Augie's Fairbanks television operation completely and decisively. The only vestige of relief was the antenna high atop the Northward Building, one of the few locations immune from the muddy waters. Damage estimates elsewhere demonstrate the severity of the disaster. The Alaska Railroad, for instance, sustained $2 million in damages, while $8 million was necessary to restore losses at Fort Wainwright.

There was no warning of impending danger. There had been some heavy rain, but the flooding came on faster than any realization of its threat. The flood came to NTV on the heals of financial commitments made as a result of the 1964 earthquake losses in Anchorage and relocation of the broadcast operation there. Only nine months earlier, the new Broadcast Center in Anchorage had opened. No other broadcast operation was hit by the flood as were KTVF-TV and KFRB radio.

The water gradually rose in the Northward Building basement. KTVF continued to operate while the power remained on to run the water pumps. But when the power finally failed, staff members were forced to flee, using lit newspapers to guide them out of the building.

A corner of the Northward building had been built on an old slough and at a soft spot in the concrete floor, all hell broke loose in a thunderous explosion of water. A fifteen foot hole in the floor gave way to a fountain-like eruption driving up all sorts of debris.

Dick Ward, who ran the drugstore on the next floor up, was one of the first to survey the damage. It was paramount that he assess the damage to pharmacy inventory, particularly chemicals and acids, as well as to secure narcotic and injectable supplies from possible vandalism. With water chest deep, a flashlight and prod in hand, he slowly entered the dismal scene. Debris of every description clung to the ooze and mud-covered furnishings and fixtures.

As he made his way into the office area, Dick felt something brush by him. He flashed his light to investigate, and emitted a blood-curdling shriek at the sight of a partially exposed body. To Dick's relief it turned out to be the stuffed Teddy bear that station manager John Griffin frequently used in his live commercials. Dick also spotted four Arctic grayling swimming in the basement waters.

The flood water at its crest reached to the top of downtown parking meters; at basement level, everything was under close to fourteen feet of muddy water. The water level dropped very slowly over the next two months as Dick, with his ten-man crew, excavated the debris with bulldozers and seven continuously operating pumps. The water was still hip deep a week later when Augie was permitted into the damaged area. Except for the clean-up crews, this was the earliest entry allowed due to safety requirements. It was the biggest mess Augie had ever seen.

At newly acquired KFRB radio on College Road, Ted Lehne was announcing when the flood waters began to rise. He announced that he was stranded and asked if someone could give him a hand. A man driving in the area with a boat in the back of his pickup heard the message, rowed out to the KFRB transmitter, and rescued Ted. By this time the water level had covered College Road and was thirty inches deep in the station building.

The flood wiped out the high voltage and modulation transformers in the 10,000-watt transmitter. The station, however, resumed broadcasts within a week with the use of its auxiliary 600-watt transmitter. A new 10,000-watt transmitter arrived and full output was restored on November 10. Interestingly, the auxiliary transmitter was the original one installed by Stan Bennett and Augie in 1939 at KFAR. It had been sold to Bill Wagner and used at KFQD radio, his Anchorage station, and subsequently transferred to KFRB. It had gotten a little wet also, but was repairable for temporary use.

The flood was ugly, dirty, and smelly. The force of the water was highly destructive, but the worst damage was the contamination from the chemicals the water transported and deposited. Pat, Augie's wife, attended to Ted Lehne, infected from polluted water, exhausted from his work and rescue, in their Anchorage home. The hard work, the stench, the exhaustion from no sleep are not forgotten by those who labored so tirelessly to restore the damage done to the Northern Television equipment.

Consulting Engineer George Frese and his wife, Augie's old friends from East Wenatchee, Washington, abbreviated their long-awaited vacation to Alaska. While his wife returned home, George volunteered to depart for

Fairbanks to apply his engineering skills in reconstruction. His experience at "drying out" transformers during the Columbia River flood affecting Portland and Vancouver, Washington, was useful in evaluating the utility of the damaged KFRB transmitter. Unfortunately, contaminants had rendered the transformers beyond saving; it was more economical to replace them than to salvage them.

The immediate concern was to get KFRB back on the air as soon as possible. George scrounged the needed transformers from hams and others around town to rehabilitate the auxiliary unit to 600 watts. That's how KFRB resumed programming so fast with its auxiliary transmitter. George had worked in the mud and muck for a week, and refused to take any pay. He philosophized that when a fellow broadcaster was in trouble, he'd do all he could to help.

Insurance coverage of $146,000 paid for a new radio transmitter and some of the television equipment. What was not provided for was a new facility. A low-interest SBA disaster loan was acquired to rebuild on the second floor of the Northward Building. Everything had to be reconstructed to accommodate the relocation to higher ground. It was also decided to move the radio station under the same broadcast roof.

Time was of the essence, and it was a major effort to get the station back on the air. For three-and-a-half months John Griffin and Sue Yoder worked to sort and order. They were the only employees salaried during this time. Other staff members remained loyal to the operation and resumed their positions gradually as reconstruction work continued and permitted their reinstatement. KTVF-TV resumed programming on December 9, 1967. For a while the skeleton staff worked out of one small, cozy office area. John Griffin's office served also for accounting, copy, and live news broadcasts while work continued on the studio and additional office space.

Color television was making its debut at the time, and a highlight of reconstruction for Augie was his announcement to bring in new color equipment. The first color conversion in Alaskan TV had been in Anchorage in 1966 by Midnight Sun, Channel 2. That was for color film. When KTVF resumed operations with color film after the flood, it forced KFAR-TV to do likewise. Live color was inaugurated in Fairbanks three years later when KTVF purchased a sound-on-film camera from CBS News. KTVF was the only station in Alaska with a state-of-the-art camera of this type. A year later the NTV Fairbanks station converted to a full-color operation, the first station to do so, with a live studio camera. Even the Anchorage stations were still shooting black and white news film.

In the post-earthquake, post-flood period came another financial burden that almost broke Augie's company. The five-year period from 1969 to 1974 was probably the lowest point in the history of Northern Television. Augie describes it as "nip and tuck."

In 1969 the networks converted from film to two-inch video tape. Therefore, Northern Television was required to purchase expensive color tape equipment for both KTVA and KTVF. There was no alternative. The debt service was now overwhelming. Two traits helped Augie hold things together—his sense of humor and his eternal optimism. To know Augie is to know that he always sees a bright side to everything. He accentuates the positive. But it is more than a positive attitude; he is undaunted by adversity. Today is today, but there is a tomorrow.

Augie probably did not laugh a lot internally during this time, but he is a proponent of "laughter is the best medicine." He loves to laugh and he loves to see other people share in the mirth. He can be a downright prankster, mischievous in his delivery of jest. In that sport he is no spectator.

(Another buttress during this difficult period was the genesis of satellite communications, which will be discussed in some detail later in this chapter.)

Of course, it took a lot more to survive, but there is a great deal within an individual's constitution that affects the outcome no matter what the odds. On more than one occasion it has been said that Augie Hiebert's leadership and vision, along with his tenacity and persistence, are responsible for the success of telecommunications in Alaska.

It is evident that Augie's driving force has been his desire to do more—to not settle for less than what would best serve the growth of communications in Alaska for all Alaskans. When so many interests are involved in the communications business, public and private, in a frontier atmosphere, developing a telecommunications policy could have been chaotic. Perhaps Augie could be likened to a musical conductor, making sure everyone marched to the beat of the same drum. Often he has interceded when the wheels of progress were spinning off track, or the marriage of government and the private sector was threatened with incompatibility.

Augie has fostered a cross-fertilization of ideas to promote the growth of telecommunications and has thereby generated enthusiasm to go forward and get the job done. Though Augie has long been in the management end of the business, he still possesses his engineer's grasp of the telecommunication possibilities for Alaska. He is a mentally athletic man and the transmission of the message is his passion. Julie Guy, former NTV staff member and deputy commissioner of telecommunications for Alaska, describes the scope of Augie's direction:

His knowledge and his ability to plan and execute major telecommunications advances for Alaska were unlimited. He engaged the whole spectrum of military, political, network, and bureaucratic leaders to further his plans. He always had a number of projects on the fire, as evidenced by the neat stacks of manila folders behind his desk filled with project documents. He prodigiously wrote letters, each advancing his plans a step at a time.

Perhaps one secret of Augie's success is his incredible filing system, and his ability to recall or find any information that's needed. Actually, Augie's filing system has been a consistent source of amusement; he never throws anything away. His files are strategically located on the desk top, credenza, surrounding floor, and chairs, never to be disturbed by anyone else. Once when Augie was out of town, Norma Goodman decided to launch a clean-up operation of the boss's office. Suffice it to say, he could find nothing when he returned to his office, now neatly organized to reflect a proper executive image.

Augie's appetite for technology was whetted by Dr. Wernher Von Braun's visit to Alaska during the summer of 1961. It was then that Alaska entered the cosmic arena, and Augie began to champion satellite communications for the state. It was to be a slow but calculated process. Americans were entering the "Space Age" as dictated by commitments made by President John F. Kennedy. The momentum in U. S. space exploration had been accelerated in response to the advances made by the Soviet Union in the 1950s. The goal of the 1960s for the United States was well defined—put a man on the moon by the end of the decade.

Dr. Von Braun was director of the National Aeronautics and Space Administration (NASA), and through the 1960s, he and his missile team developed the successful Redstone Rockets and the Saturn rockets used in the manned lunar landing program. They also began the Skylab research and development program which included a manned earth-orbiting system, moon information retrieval vehicles, and space transportation shuttle system. Dr. Von Braun was a visionary of space potentials and full utilization of satellite capabilities.

The Civil Air Patrol (CAP) invited Dr. Von Braun to Alaska to promote aerospace education throughout the state. Lt. Col. Bob Livesay, an Air Force officer in charge of CAP, appropriately asked Augie to arrange for and manage Dr. Von Braun's Alaskan itinerary.

Dr. Von Braun conducted seminars for young people about the early stages of the Space Age. He touched everyone with whom he was in contact, civilian and military alike. He was a true teacher, as anxious to learn as his pupils. His unassuming and mild-mannered nature contributed to his likability. His brilliance, articulation, and sense of humor were a testament to his professional position with NASA and a credit to our space program. He was a gentle giant.

Dr. Von Braun's itinerary included numerous side trips. He was escorted via an Alaskan Air Command plane to the University of Alaska in Fairbanks, where he toured the facilities and conferred with professors on aerospace matters. From there Dr. Von Braun was flown to Point Barrow to visit the Naval Arctic Research Laboratory. From Point Barrow, he was flown by helicopter to a Coast Guard Icebreaker and witnessed action through the Arctic ice flow. And there were fishing trips here and there as well. It was no doubt his success at fishing that brought Von Braun back to Alaska in 1974.

The paths of two pioneer spirits had crossed—that of Dr. Wernher Von Braun and that of Augie Hiebert. The seed was planted and ready for nurturing.

During the summer of 1964, Augie made two far-reaching commitments to the future of broadcasting in Alaska. The first appeared as a front page story in the *Anchorage Daily Times*, July 6, 1964. The announcement was made that NTV had acquired shares in the Communications Satellite Corporation (COMSAT). The stock was purchased as a demonstration of faith in satellite communications as an investment in Alaska's future.

The other commitment was the organization of the Alaska Broadcaster's Association (ABA) of which Augie was first president, a post he held for three consecutive years. Alvin O. Bramstedt, Sr. was cofounder. Augie's main reason for organizing the ABA was to lay the groundwork for satellite communications. As Augie saw it, a structured group could better attract interest in satellite communications in Alaska. A unified coalition could accomplish more than broadcasters working individually for the same purpose.

Sitting around the Hiebert dining table with a handful of other interested parties, Ted Stevens, an Anchorage attorney, proceeded to draft the by-laws and articles of incorporation for the Alaska Broadcaster's Association.

One of the first problems the new organization tackled was the Alaska Communications System (ACS) rate structure for radio news procurement. Rates were high, and it was felt that if the rates were reduced to a reasonable level, it would help not only the broadcasters but also ACS; more people could afford to use the service. The resultant reduced rates were beneficial to all, and ACS tripled its business within a year.

By the summer of 1967 the American Consortium Company and only U.

S. satellite carrier, COMSAT, had established satellite earth stations all over the world by virtue of their international partnership with Intelsat. Communication satellite technology was progressing at a rapid and serviceable rate.

That year also marked Alaska's Centennial, and in June, during his last year as ABA president, Augie invited two high-ranking men—Rosel Hyde, FCC chairman, and retired Major General George Sampson, vice-president of operations for COMSAT—to speak at the ABA annual meeting in Fairbanks. Both men were escorted throughout the state to witness the status of communications in Alaska. They were favorably impressed and acknowledged their confidence that satellite technology could be utilized to serve the communication needs of Alaska. A satellite that would permit live television broadcasting to Alaska was already in orbit around the earth. All that was needed was a ground station to make the broadcasts a reality.

(Augie learned early on that the only way for people who needed to know what communication problems in Alaska were all about was to actually show them. Those who Augie has guided through the state have departed with amplified trust in Augie's efforts to expand on communications in his far north outpost. Augie has deliberately and diligently labored to achieve this credibility, and when he is referred to as Mr. Alaska in Washington D.C., it reflects his status as the representative of all Alaska broadcasters.)

While organizing the June 1967 ABA meeting, Augie came up with the idea to commemorate the Centennial Year with the first satellite transmission in Alaska, at Fairbanks. Augie talked over the idea with Senator E. L. (Bob) Bartlett who, until his untimely death in December 1968, worked with Augie to promote satellite communications for Alaska. Senator Bartlett was in full agreement, and proceeded to turn the exploratory wheels. NASA had portable earth station equipment and COMSAT had the satellite in place. Senator

Bartlett sent a letter to NASA inquiring about the possibilities of getting their earth station to Fairbanks for the first demonstration transmission. Time went by and NASA failed to answer. Augie was in Washington, D. C., at the time, and he and Senator Bartlett decided they should call NASA to see what was up. Bartlett called the NASA representatives to his office and pointedly asked them, "Since when does an agency that the legislature funds ignore a letter sent by a voting member of the U. S. Senate? Since when?"

The senator's remarks achieved the desired response, and the first satellite demonstration in Alaska was scheduled for August 15. No one could have predicted the events that would derail the project. The Six-Day War in the Middle East occurred in June, and military priority preempted transport of the NASA earth station to Alaska.

But as fate would have it, the Chena River flooded on August 15. NASA must have been pleased because they really didn't want to send the equipment to Alaska, and Augie was happy not to have witnessed half-a-million dollars worth of equipment floating down the Chena River.

In three short years Alaska did have an earth station. No grass grew under the feet of Gen. George Sampson. Upon his return to Washington, D.C., from Alaska, he organized a task force to research the suitability of an earth station in Alaska. The road ahead was bumpy but not impassable, thanks to Augie's vigilance. In March 1968 COMSAT sent their expert investigatory team to Alaska to assess the financial viability of an earth station, and in April the COMSAT board of directors approved a proposal to build the earth station somewhere between Anchorage and Fairbanks. Talkeetna, ninety miles north of Anchorage, was selected as the best location for the ground station facility.

In response to a growing interest in satellite communications, Governor Walter J. Hickel, on April 2, 1968, announced the appointment of a seven-member Satellite Communication Task Force with Augie as its chairman. The task force's prime function was to work in liaison with COMSAT officials coordinating efforts by potential military, state, industrial, and educational users in support of an Alaskan earth station. The station would link Alaska with the international satellite complex (INTELSAT) in successful operation in the Pacific. This link would connect Alaska with the South 48, Hawaii, Japan, the South Pacific, and eventually the world.

In late November the task force invited COMSAT Chairman James McCormack and his staff to meet with Gov. Hickel and the state delegation. At this meeting a resolution was drafted to be forwarded to FCC Chairman Rosel Hyde urging a positive response to the pending COMSAT earth station application. One member of the state delegation was conspicuously absent. Senator Bob Bartlett was too ill to attend. (Senator Bartlett's written message, which was read to the meeting, is included in the Appendix.)

On December 6, 1968, COMSAT submitted to the FCC its formal application for the construction of a satellite earth station at Talkeetna. It was shortly thereafter that Senator Bob Bartlett died, and Augie began his relentless and lengthy campaign to name the earth station in his honor.

Governor Hickel was at this time preparing to assume his appointed position of secretary of interior in the Nixon administration. One of his parting official state duties was the appointment of Ted Stevens to fill the void left in our nation's capitol. Senator Stevens was predisposed to perpetuate the legacy of Senator Bartlett in telecommunications for Alaska. As a member of the Senate Subcommittee on Communications, Senator Stevens has maintained a working relationship with the FCC and has been counseled on Alaskan telecommunications by the expert himself, Augie Hiebert.

Between the December 6, 1968, filing and the May 14, 1969, approval of a construction permit, COMSAT encountered significant opposition. Two "landline" telephone companies, Glacier State and Continental Telephone, protested that COMSAT rates would be excessive and that the existing landline system should be upgraded and maintained. When Congress instructed the Air Force to sell the Alaska Communications System (ACS), there arose the additional controversy that COMSAT should not be permitted to construct the earth station until finalization of the ACS sale since the buyer of ACS would be the common carrier for the earth station transmissions systems operation. The Department of Defense withdrew its initial approval, expressed in a letter to the FCC toward the end of January 1969, citing the pending ACS sale and rates as substantive issues to be reviewed through a hearing process.

Since the construction season in Alaska is abbreviated by weather, time was of the essence for permit approval to insure completion of the project by the summer of 1970. As chairman of the Governor's Satellite Communications Task Force, Augie used his authority to counter the opposition. Armed with detailed information to support the earth station, information prepared primarily by Augie himself, Senator Stevens met with Secretary of Defense Melvin Laird. As a result of the meeting, the Department of Defense withdrew its dissenting motion, as did Glacier State and Continental Telephone, and COMSAT's permit application was approved. Construction of Alaska's first earth station at Talkeetna began in the spring of 1969.

About this time, Augie was preparing for his annual stockholders meeting. In 1969 the meeting date coincided with the Anchorage Chamber of Commerce Gold Pan Awards Banquet. It took a lot of fast talking, but Al Shewe, NTV sales, and Bev Rova Miller, Augie's secretary, convinced him that the annual stockholders meeting be postponed. The next step was to convince Augie that he should attend the Chamber Banquet. The ploy worked without suspicion. When Augie was called up to receive the prestigious Gold Pan Award, he was the most surprised person in the room. A master of strategy himself, he had been outfoxed by the unsuspected maneuvering. The inscription on the Gold Pan Award reads: "Augie Hiebert, Pioneer in Alaska Satellite Communications." It occupies a prominent place in his office, which is filled with many tributes and honors.

On July 21, 1969, during the initial phase of construction for the earth station, Alaska had its first taste of what satellite communications was all about. Alaska joined the rest of the nation, the rest of the world, in witnessing Neal Armstrong make his historic lunar footprints. Through the energetic efforts of Alaska's congressional delegation, Secretary of Defense Laird approved the use of a military mobile ground station and satellite to bring the live lunar landing coverage to Anchorage. Anchorage swelled with the influx of people from outside the city who came to view the historic event. Alaska Airlines provided reduced fares from Fairbanks to Anchorage, a $39.90 special package, for the week of the broadcast.

The CBS network feed with Walter Cronkite as anchor was broadcast over all three local stations: KENI-TV, Channel 2; KHAR-TV, Channel 13; and KTVA-TV, Channel 11, the CBS-affiliated station. Augie coordinated the network feed to the local stations through his CBS affiliation. His dream had come true.

The live broadcast itself was a technical miracle. The military satellite used had never relayed television broadcasts. To reproduce a live picture to Alaska beamed from a satellite not intended to broadcast to Alaska, the relay had to be made at an awkward angle. In addition, the broadcast had to be converted from civilian to military and back to civilian frequencies. The most unique technical challenge for local engineers was synchronizing the video and audio portions of the telecast, which were fed separately. Video was fed over the military satellite, while the audio portion was brought by a more direct route via ACS. Since the audio was received a fifth of a second earlier than the video, it was necessary for local stations to delay the audio so that both picture and sound would synchronize. The diagram depicts the circuitous path necessary for Alaska to receive the live signal.

Augie expressed his delight with the telecast in a press release following the live coverage: "I had no idea that we were going to get this kind of quality on a circuit like this that was put together at the last minute and not designed for civilian television in the first place. I think the military did a fantastic job." It truly was incredible to see a clear live picture of the moon landing that sunny July weekend. For Walter Cronkite, it was a marathon broadcast. Locally, thirty hours of continuous coverage was provided on July 20 and 21. Live broadcasts extended from the July 16 launch to splash down on July 21.

• • •

Errata

The following diagram should have been reproduced on page 134:

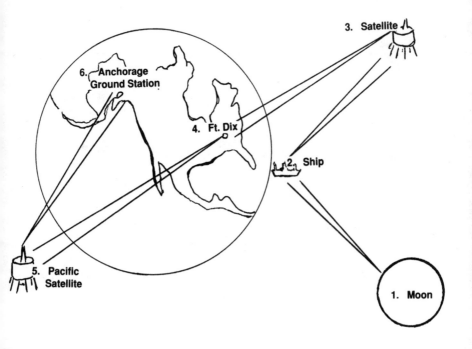

In addition, some items that should have been in the Appendix
were inadvertently left out. These will be added in the next printing.

In late 1969 seventy Alaskans from various parts of the state participated in a policy conference held in Anchorage and conducted by the Brookings Institution of Washington, D.C. The purpose of the conference was to sift through opinions and draw up guidelines and recommendations for the legislature on the use of Alaska's new oil riches—oil riches resulting from the Prudhoe Bay/North Slope discovery and $900 million lease sale.

The "think tank" precipitated free-wheeling talk and, among other subjects, a keen interest in communications. In response to conference needs, Augie prepared a paper titled "Anatomy of Alaska's Telecommunications Satellite in Alaska's Immediate Future.". Augie distilled other seminar discussions into a paper that described what telecommunications and satellite use should be. In the paper, Augie gave the following reasons for establishing a state telecommunications policy:

There is an urgent need for fully adequate telecommunications services of all kinds.

The seminars have eloquently revealed the central role of telecommunications in all phases of Alaskan development—economic, social, and cultural.

Alaska is at the communications crossroads with an unparalleled opportunity to shape the future.

The state is actively seeking to identify and establish the policies and the objectives which will lead it into the most desirable future.

No other state or country of the developed world has had the opportunity to proceed to the crest of economic and social explosion using a telecommunications system whose great cost did not have to be amortized before a new stage of development could be initiated.

On June 30, 1970, Talkeetna earth station was dedicated in honor and in memory of Senator Bob Bartlett. The ceremonies, conducted in the silhouette of Mt. McKinley and the Talkeetna Range, were as majestic as their setting. An earth station traditionally is named for a local identifying geographic feature, not for a person. COMSAT, however, was agreeable to Augie's idea of naming the facility after Senator Bartlett. For fifteen months Augie promoted his idea to the state bureaucracy. The first go around with the state legislature in 1969 bore no fruit. Letters were then sent to each state senator and representative proposing that a small lake near the ground station site be named Bartlett Lake, thereby providing the geographic basis for dedication. But the lake had already been named Christiansen Lake, for the well-known bush pilot Haaken Christiansen. On March 23, 1970, Augie submitted to the Alaska State Geographic Board an application to name the rolling hills along the border just east of COMSAT's site as Bartlett Hills.

Within a week the legislature proclaimed the rolling hills as Bartlett Ridge and requested that the earth station be named Bartlett Earth Station. On March 27 the resolution was signed into law by Governor Keith Miller. This was only one short month before the planned dedication ceremonies.

During the ceremony, all watched under the sunny skies as Mrs. Vide Bartlett, wife of the late senator, "pushed the button" to consummate the dedication. When the button was pushed, a signal shot 22,300 miles to the Intelsat III satellite and back to the earth station where it activated the explosive device that cut the red, white, and blue ribbons attached to the earth station dish.

Throughout the day, Augie coordinated the satellite transmissions from Tokyo, Guam, and Hawaii for use in a composite program simulcast later that evening on KENI-TV and KTVA-TV. Lowell Thomas, Jr., emceed the program which also included highlights of the dedicatory ceremony and a taped message from President Nixon. The incoming live transmission from Tokyo held a special reward for Augie. His daughter Peggy, one of the two official Alaska hostesses at the Alaskan Exhibit, Expo '70, in Osaka, had traveled by bullet train to Tokyo to participate in the first live satellite transmission to Alaska. Outgoing satellite signals beamed blanket tossing, gold panning, and conversations with Alaskans to millions of Japanese viewers via NET, a Japanese educational network.

The Bartlett Earth Station, the farthest north of its kind in the satellite communications system, was one of eight such facilities in the United States. The huge dish, ninety-eight-feet in diameter, atop its sixteen-foot concrete pedestal is a breathtaking sight. The pedestal serves as the control facility for the operation. The antenna structure, standing the height of a ten-story building and weighing 315 tons, can be rotated rapidly at one degree per second, and precisely track, within two one-hundredths of a degree, a satellite stationed at 22,300 miles altitude.

Communication signals received from a satellite are only a fraction of a watt in power—mere space whispers—by the time they reach the earth station. Here they are amplified a million fold or more, funneled by the antenna into supersensitive receiver-amplifiers, again boosted in power, then further processed through the station. These receiver-amplifiers are cooled by helium to temperatures near absolute zero to minimize molecular noise that might interfere with the quality of the faint incoming signals.

For outgoing signals, the antenna transmits information at the same time to the satellite on a different frequency, concentrating these signals into extremely accurate, narrow beams.

Centralized operation of the station is handled in the control building, which houses a maze of sophisticated equipment. A unique feature of the Bartlett Earth Station is the location of major electronic and control facilities in the circular concrete structure directly beneath the antenna. This compactness pays off in the greater ease of maintenance and reduced operating costs. The station is manned around the clock by a staff of sixteen.

Microwave links were constructed by COMSAT at Talkeetna, Twelve-Mile, and Scotty Lakes. The facility is supplied with uninterrupted power by four fully automatic 225-kilowatt diesel generators.

The Bartlett Earth Station is capable of sending all types of high quality communications including multiple-channel telephone, telegraph, facsimile, data, and black and white and color television. The eighty telephone circuit immediately enhanced telephone service from Alaska to the Lower 48. The utilization of the operation for inclusive live television service would require an evolution of integrated systems and the maturation of the technical aspects of the industry.

This marked the beginning of a new era in telecommunications in Alaska. Fresh challenges lay ahead for coordinating and applying satellite technology to its best use. Rural Alaska would become a testing ground for global modeling.

Augie and Norma Goodman at reception for her Gold Mike Award, 1960.

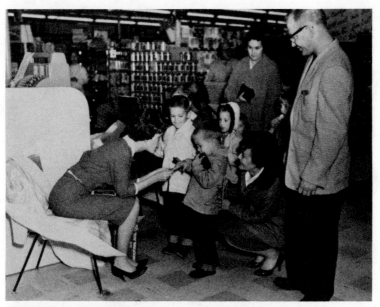

"Romper Room's" Miss Carolyn (Carolyn Guess) discusses the many advantages of being a DO-BEE to children at a local Anchorage merchant's mall, where she was guest celebrity.

Photo by Augie Hiebert

A proud Dr. Wernher Von Braun posing with his "trophy" Lake Trout with Dan Cuddy to his left, and Ward Gay and Lt. Gen. Frank Armstrong to his right, Lake Clark, July 1961.

Augie and Dr. Wernher Von Braun. Are they discussing the future of satellite communications in Alaska . . . or the big fish that didn't get away?!

McKinley Building after Great Alaska Earthquake, March 27, 1964.

Charles Hickman receiving Certificate of Appreciation for contribution to Radio Free Europe fundraising by Augie, RFE fund project manager for Alaska (circa, 1965).

Photo by Franklin W. Butte

Putting the pieces together, like a giant erector set, the new 392-foot multiple use (AM, FM, TV) tower at Broadcast Center in Spenard, Anchorage, is assembled on sit, fall 1966.

Augie's first look at Fairbanks flood damage, August 31, 1967, KTVF,
Northward Building basement.

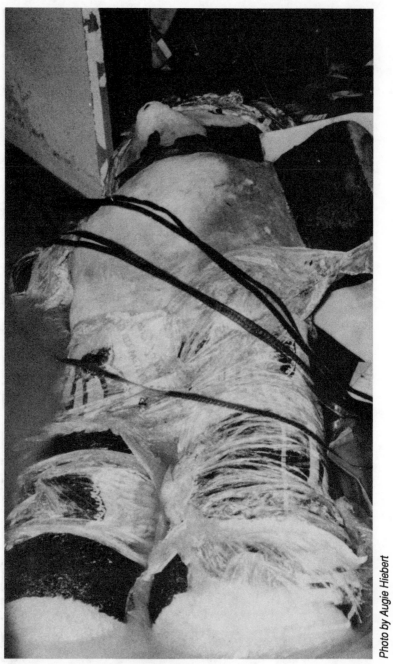

A flood casualty—John Giffin's giant teddy

Chena River muck and ooze cover control room
equipment at KTVF, Fairbanks.

Bartlett Earth Station at Talkeetna, seemingly dwarfed by the majesty of Mt. McKinley, June 1970.

CHAPTER 5

BEAM ME DOWN, SCOTTY!

T he progress of telecommunications in Alaska in the 1970s could be likened to riding a roller coaster for the first time—thrilling! There was anticipation and enthusiasm for applying to the broadcast media technological innovations from space exploration. Broadcast of the moonwalk was an affirmation of the capabilities. Politicians were seeing the potential of a good cause to offer to their constituents. Alaska provided a unique source for innovation in broadcast technology and application.

The eight years following the earthquake, flood, and investments in equipment were taking their toll on Augie Hiebert. He had mortgaged his personal property to fund the tape conversion. For him it was a daily struggle for survival. Predictions of a better economy remained hopes barren of fruit. A contemplative man, Augie expressed empathy for his father in a letter to his mother in March 1972:

> How many times I have wished that I could turn back the clock, with the experience I have now, and just tell him that now I understand what he was doing and why. He did it because it had to be done, and one cannot turn aside from the course he sets when he knows it is right, regardless of the

consequences. He lighted one light rather than to curse the darkness; and if this philosophy of his has in any way been inherited by me, I'm mighty proud of it.

As dark as his days must have seemed, his lights were illuminating the way to a brighter future for Alaska.

Augie's view of satellite communications dates back to his early radio days in Fairbanks. In his words, "Satellite technology was invented for Alaska." Satellite transmission is not subject to auroral magnetic disturbances (fade outs) like lower frequencies; when a satellite is placed in a geostationary orbit, it sees all of Alaska. Therefore, communications could reach the people in rural areas of Alaska who were most affected by the northern phenomenon. At KFAR Augie got a sense for the meaning of reliable communications, not only for its entertainment value, but also for its ability to serve emergency needs. Augie also had a sensitivity to the benefits of modernization, such as health services and education. Even today there are not doctors in every village, but there is the telecommunications capability—anywhere, anytime—to obtain immediate expert medical advice.

There were skeptics when it came to satellite potential for Alaska, and there were those who did not understand that it should apply to all Alaskans. Augie set out to prove that it would work and it would work for everyone. If the capabilities were available for everyone, they should be utilized for everyone. That was the bottom line.

When the Bartlett Earth Station came on line in July 1970, the Governor's Satellite Communications Task Force Augie chaired was disbanded. Its purpose had been fulfilled. There was now no agency to adequately deal with satellite communication and technological developments in telecommunications in Alaska. Few people were able to conceptualize what modern telecommunications in Alaska could accomplish.

To fill the void, the Alaska Educational Broadcasting Commission (AEBC) appointed a Telecommunications Advisory Committee with Augie as its chairman. This committee helped establish the policies and procedures for the state agency within the executive branch known as the Office of Telecommunications.

A system had to be in place that would allow urban-to-urban, bush-to-bush, bush-to-urban, and urban-to-bush communications. It all had to be tied together. If a proposal could not cover all of Alaska, then it did not offer a system that should be allowed to come to Alaska. Augie's objectives for a comprehensive approach to telecommunications management are best expressed in a statement he presented on July 10, 1970, to the Alaska Public Service Commission during hearings conducted prior to the RCA Alascom transfer. It is a speech impassioned by a dedication, commitment, and conceptualization of what could and should be done. The following is an excerpt (see the Appendix for the full text):

> Satellite communications offer the bright promise to accomplish the philosophy and infinite benefits to a total Alaskan Telecommunications System. A satellite—in geostationary orbit 22,300 miles distant from the earth—will illuminate every Alaskan city and village, offering equal opportunity for all Alaskans to communicate in whatever mode of transmission suits their needs and requirements. The sociological, economic, and educational benefits are obvious and need no amplification here.

Alaska has an uncommon opportunity; the Alaska Public Service Commission bears an unparalleled responsibility to at once guide and protect the destiny of what can become the model telecommunications system of the world. The economic, social, technological factors are all present—the timing is perfect—the scenario can be, and must be written to provide for adequate communications wherever there are Alaskans who need to communicate within our state. Someone must speak for the isolated villages; someone must be concerned about opening the window on the world educationally to those who have been exposed by our society to the urban way of life, and now must learn to cope with it. Someone with policy making powers and judicial wisdom must care about Alaskans outside the mainstream of advantages we take for granted. . . .

• • •

"I was a green kid fresh from Philly when I first met Augie," said Tom Busch, manager of KNOM radio in Nome. That was on February 3, 1970, Tom's first full day in Alaska. It was to be the beginning of a long and enriched professional and personal relationship for them both. Augie had been coordinating the legal and engineering work for Father Jim Poole's dream, a radio station in Nome. Tom was the noncommercial station's first engineer and a volunteer—as was the entire staff. He was called to Alaska to install and maintain the equipment for the new station. Tom relates how "Augie was unimaginably busy, but he swept everything aside for several hours in order to bring me up to speed on what was happening with the Nome application. Throughout the first year of KNOM's construction, Augie worked in every way he could to make the project easy for us."

Except for a short stint in Fairbanks as engineer at KIAK, Tom has remained with KNOM. As many have done, Tom too has joined the ranks of engineer gone manager. Therein he has shaped KNOM, serving all of Northwest Alaska with 10,000 watts of power, into an award winning public service radio station. KNOM's vigilant coverage of the Iditarod Trail Sled Dog Race from Anchorage to Nome has become as much of an Alaskan tradition as the race itself.

Having joined the fraternity of Alaskan broadcasters, Tom has garnered the respect of his fellow colleagues as ABA president in 1982 and the Association's "Broadcaster of the Year" in 1986.

• • •

On January 3, 1971, Anchorage residents saw their first commercial live telecast from outside Alaska on KTVA. It was the National Football Conference championship game, live and in color, between the Dallas Cowboys and the San Francisco 49ers. The game was the first live via satellite commercial program to be sent through the Bartlett Earth Station, dedicated only six months earlier. Augie underscored the importance of this broadcast when he told the *Anchorage Daily Times*, "This is really a significant event for Alaska because now we have entered an age in television which the other 49 states have had for some time."

The broadcast was a first but it was the last commercial television transmission for the Alaska Communications System (ACS) which on January 10, 1971, was turned over to RCA Alascom.

The first live satellite television transmission originating inside Alaska to the Lower 48 would follow shortly, also over KTVA, the CBS affiliate. The historic broadcast of the Department of Interior's Environmental Impact Hearings on the Trans-Alaska oil pipeline occurred on February 24, 1971. The Trans-Alaska pipeline was a turning point for Alaska. The economic consequence has impacted every Alaskan, then and now, boom and bust. And KTVA and CBS knew the significance of the satellite feed of the hearings to the rest of the nation, beating the competition by twenty-four hours! (The CBS newsrelease describing the historic significance of the broadcast is included in the Appendix.)

The eyes of the world were on Alaska on numerous occasions of historical and national importance in the early 1970s. On September 26, 1971, President Richard M. Nixon and Japan's Emperor Hirohito met in Anchorage. It was the first time any ruling Japanese emperor had set foot on American soil. The meeting was also the first ever between the heads of state of the two nations.

A consortium pool was set up to feed media coverage of the event via satellite to the three networks. KTVA participated in the pool, but added live coverage over radio KBYR and KNIK-FM in Anchorage and KTVF-TV and KFRB radio in Fairbanks, by means of an exclusive microwave link.

On February 28, 1972, CBS News celebrated another first for them and KTVA. "The CBS Evening News with Walter Cronkite" originated from KTVA in Anchorage. "The Evening News" normally originates from New York; rarely is the location altered unless the occasion is of national significance. On this occasion, President Nixon had arrived in Anchorage in the dark of winter's cold early morning hours on his return trip from Peking, China and his historic meetings with Premier Chou En-Lai. RCA had a satellite earth station in Peking, and KTVA had live telecasts of Nixon in Peking throughout the week of what was called "the journey for peace" to Communist China.

The CBS News executives in New York decided it was imperative to originate the "Evening News" broadcast with Walter Cronkite, Eric Severeid, and White House correspondent Dan Rather on the scene in Anchorage. Events of the historic trip were fed live via satellite to the "Evening News" in New York from the KTVA back lot.

Alaska was moving into her own place in the world, rather than being removed from it by her remoteness, having borne the burden as an incongruity to the Continental United States for so long. Augie was influential in correcting the misconceptions about Alaska he frequently encountered outside the state. He was vital to CBS News in this regard, and to the other small market affiliate fraternity where his adaptability to growing markets set a pattern observed in the Lower 48.

In June 1971 Augie and Pat were in Los Angeles for the CBS affiliate conference and fall preview. Augie had been named to the board of directors of the CBS Television Network Affiliates Association. He was elected to the position by the management of the sixteen stations in the western stations at-large district. Prior to his election to the board, he was an active member of the CBS Affiliate Satellite Transmission Committee. The small market affiliates were allied, on both coasts, to facilitate a louder voice and avoid getting lost in the shuffle. The annual meetings in November, the onset of winter in Alaska, were staged in Hawaii, the Virgin Islands, and Puerto Rico. Augie and Pat would have to endure two weeks of sand and surf in November for the next three years.

(The 1970s was a period of growth, and the Hiebert household was no exception with the addition of two sons-in-law and three grandchildren.)

What was achieved in telecommunications in Alaska in six short years transcends the imagination. The accomplishments—from low-power videotape transmission experiments by AEBC in 1971-1972 to a satellite demonstration to twenty-three Alaskan villages in 1977— were slow and laborious but sure. Many were involved, but few knew of the trials and tribulations. Augie was a catalyst and the work horse for unprecedented approvals by the commercial networks and the FCC.

The concept of Mini-TV (i.e., low-power television) was born within the Alaska Educational Broadcasting Commission when Augie was a member around 1970. Augie takes no credit for its birth, but he was an active participant, a foster parent, in its growth, direction, and widespread utilization.

The idea was to reach villages beyond the range of translator facilities originating from local television stations. In a sense the function was that of a translator, but the operation differed from a translator in that the signal is not taken off the air and converted from one frequency to another. The signal is received from a video tape and then transmitted to individual televisions sets. The power is only 10 watts and the installation resembles a "mini" TV station. The phrase was coined in Alaska and has been used ever since to describe the system.

There was no precedent for licensing with the FCC. Mini-TV was licensed as a translator, but for all practical purposes a new procedure for paperwork had to be created and a routine established for Mini-TV licensing with the FCC.

Mini-TV was first demonstrated at two locations in Alaska in late 1971 to early 1972 through the University of Alaska's Division of Media Services under the direction of Dr. Charles M. Northrip. The experimental Mini-TV project at Fort Yukon and Angoon was under Special Temporary Authority of the FCC. Because of the experimental nature of the program, it was conducted through the local schools. It was important to diminish the temptation of villagers to buy TV sets of their own prematurely.

Different manufacturers of equipment participated in the demonstration. Bennett Engineering,. which sold Emcee technical equipment, was one of them. Stan Bennett, Augie's long-time colleague and friend, had established his own company in the early 1970s and remained a responsive innovator in Alaskan broadcast projects. Stan tells of how the first Mini-TVs were handmade transmitters. There had been no market. The market for Mini-TV really developed in Alaska. Stan sold the first Mini-TV in Alaska, the first on an experimental basis at Fort Yukon, then with regularly licensed FCC authorization at St. Paul and Unalaska. Initially Emcee was the only manufacturer to design and offer Mini-TV on a commercial basis.

The successful project was accomplished through Corporation for Public Broadcasting funding and later serviced by programming from the public broadcast TV stations, dubbed to cassette format by KYUK-TV in Bethel. The experimental project led to the establishment of pilot sites at Fort Yukon, St. Paul, and Unalaska in 1973. The pilots were to be evaluated and recommendations made for expansion of the program to additional village sites.

The Mini-TV concept brought television into village homes heretofore without access to TV, thus providing entertainment and instructional services. Marv Weatherly was Bob Arnold's assistant and technical director within the AEBC in 1973. He installed the first Mini-TVs at St. Paul and Unalaska. At St. Paul the airline had lost his bag filled with two weeks of cassette tape programming. He had one tape of a PBS show on ice skating at Rockefeller Center. But that was okay; the village people was enraptured with TV.

• • •

Note should be made here of NTV alumni emerging as integral participants in State telecommunications in the dynamic stages of its development.

HILARY HILSCHER, a born and bred Alaskan and daughter of pioneer Alaskans Herb and Miriam Hilscher, commenced her illustrious career in broadcast journalism and marketing at KTVA in the news department. She was fresh out of college, the University of Missouri. As first woman news anchor in Anchorage at NTV in 1972, she recall's Augie's attitude toward news as "what affects people where they live." The next two years, 1973 and 1974, Hilary was staff assistant to Senator Ted Stevens in Washington, D.C., specifically oriented to communications issues. There was a great deal of contact at this time with Stevens's office relative to communications satellite utilization in Alaska, especially the NASA, ATS series. In 1975 Hilary returned to Alaska and was an assistant to the State Office of Telecommunications Director, Marv Weatherly, in Juneau.

GEORGE SHAGINAW filled the same deputy position under the directorship of Robert Wolp in 1976. George was chief engineer at KTVF in Fairbanks from 1965 to 1967. In 1973 he joined the State Office of Telecommunications where his expertise in technical direction was utilized in the development and execution of the State's satellite demonstration project. In the late 1970s George joined another NTV alumni, Tom Jensen, in an executive capacity at Alascom.

TOM JENSEN, also born and raised in Alaska, was involved at KFRB radio in Fairbanks from 1970 to 1974, a dynamic period of resurrection of the station to a number one spot. The key to his success was personalization of the station and community involvement and participation. From 1974 to 1976 Tom worked radio news and managed operations, along with TV news at the Broadcast Center in

Anchorage. In 1976 he joined Alascom in his present capacity as "Chief Cook" for Public Affairs. On his professional resume Tom includes, "Member NTV Alumni Association."

MEL SATHER, Alaska born and bred and owner of his own engineering consulting firm, Octagon, recounts some of his own NTV alumni history:

I came to work for Augie in the winter of 1959. The news department at KTVA needed someone to run and maintain the film processor, keep the stock of 16mm film used for news, and perform other part-time tasks suited to a high school student. Little did I know that this love-hate relationship with the film processor would span nearly a decade.

My first encounter was with then news director Peter Herford. A ten-minute interview resulted in what I was later to find was a melding into a "family," a relationship which spanned fourteen years.

I was then confronted with Jack Walden, the infamous technical director, who perfunctorily hustled me into Augie's office and waved the "new hire" in front of this guy who reminded me of Mr. Dithers, Dagwood Bumstead's boss, an impression that hasn't dimmed much over nearly thirty years.

I quickly found that television (which I had never seen until a few months previous) was far from the glamour that was envisioned for this infant industry, but that it was always challenging and interesting. Sometimes too challenging. It seemed I could do nothing right, and disaster followed in my wake—like the time I dropped a gallon of sulfuric acid on the basement floor and the fire department had to come to our rescue. Or the time I edited the entire Sunday morning baseball game backward, with all the commercial inserts "tails out." Or the time, years later in our new facility in Spenard, that I rewound an entire five hour videotape with audio on the air full blast. Augie even had time to drive to the station before it finished winding.

One can only assume there was some redeeming value in what I did, or that I was terribly amusing to have around. At any rate, I was tolerated, tutored, cajoled, and influenced by everyone at NTV. I was later to realize that Augie had a unique perspective toward young people in the new frontier of television, which today is reflected in the Augie Hiebert Scholarship. His encouragement of youthful involvement in such projects as "The Varsity Show" was to underscore a commitment to training youth in a youthful medium.

Augie is ever the pioneer, with the traditional vision of the grizzled prospector falling by the wayside, giving way to an adventurous explorer of new frontiers. His background in engineering was undoubtedly a positive influence in the quest for new technology. When I came to NTV in 1959, the station was six years old, still state-of-the-art, and as impressive looking to the newcomer as any science fiction scene from Buck Rogers. The investment in television technology wasn't the end but the beginning of Augie's quest to use new technology to improve the quality of Anchorage life.

The late sixties was a period of change for NTV, but also growth of the industry and for many of us involved in it. By this time, NTV had acquired KBYR-AM, which had a long and ignoble history in Alaskan broadcasting. Ron Moore was brought on board and his direction resulted in KBYR briefly holding forth as number one in the market with an aggressive rock format. Augie didn't much like this kind of music, and it was obvious that, at least to him, principle was more important than profit. The format slipped back into its old niche, one notch behind the police radio in popularity.

Augie had embarked upon a new, and to many of our minds, slightly bizarre adventure. He was attempting to introduce, of all things, public broadcasting into the fray. Augie was always on the "cutting edge" of new activities, such as satellite broadcasting, becoming one of the original Comsat stockholders. We were right alongside the other stations in broadcasting live via portable satellite earth station the landing of the Eagle on the moon. (In fact, Jeff Bowden and I rigged a tape delay for the landbound audio to match the video, much to the consternation of the other stations who thought we were getting a different feed than they.) But this public broadcasting thing was a horse on a different course. It was a concept in its infancy, a few years old in the rest of the country. It was an evolution from something known as "community radio" and television . . . run more from the perspective of a new idealism than the profit, mass appeal motive of commercial broadcasting. It had been formalized to the extent that a new public corporation was formed by the government to fund these alternative stations. Augie had decided that the quality of life in the last frontier could stand another boost in culture and information which would not be possible on his or any other commercial station.

Several of us were cajoled by Augie into forming a technical committee to plan the facilities for a new public television station. We formulated the first plan for a new television facility which would be designed from the ground up with "blue sky" as the objective. . . .

There are very few of the old guard in this business, especially engineering, who didn't "do time" at one facility or another of NTV. No one has ever left without taking some pearl of wisdom, or experiencing growth or change. Not everyone was sent off with champagne and well-wishes, but they all left some tattered legacy. Some have gone on to blaze their own paths, unmindful of the booster rocket that Augie, his staff, and the entity that is NTV provided. For many it may have merely been a stopping off place, good for a few paychecks, and for others, myself included, it was an indelible part of my formative years, and lay the foundation for attitudes and ideals to be developed in years to come. Augie taught those of us who paid attention what and how to do many things. Also how not to do many things. The essential ideals and attitudes that Augie Hiebert exemplified were deeply etched and are never to be altered. One may choose not to believe in his methodology in a particular instance, or one may choose to embrace an ideology learned at the master's knee, but the point of reference will always be there as a guide. At least for me.

• • •

The major controversy in satellite communications in Alaska in the early 1970s was the size of the receiver dish. The ninety-foot diameter Bartlett Earth Station antenna was simply too large and not cost effective for many locations in Alaska where populations are small and villages few and far between . . . but where communications are infinitely vital.

RCA Globcom (Alascom), the newly established operator for communications services in Alaska, was responsible for expanding satellite utilization within the state, as mandated by their purchase contract. RCA wanted to use a ten-meter dish installed in the main gateway cities, along with a small power satellite. They would effectively cream off the heavy telephone circuit concentration, leaving the smaller village areas devoid of reliable telecommunications services.

For Augie the solution was simple: prove that the small aperture (sixteen-foot diameter) dish would work in Alaska. Utilization of the smaller model would require a higher powered satellite, but he knew the proper resources and had access to the technology. It was his equal opportunity, equal access platform that he used to argue his point—"or else Alaska would always be where we'd always been before and that's a stepchild as far as telecommunications is concerned; because we just had to close the gap between distances." No one else could see Alaska like the satellites—and Augie—could see Alaska. He would not tolerate the adoption of the inferior system submitted by RCA.

When the issue of dish size surfaced, Augie made immediate contact with COMSAT officials to explore the possibilities of transporting to Alaska the sixteen-foot (4.5 meter) dish earth station he had seen outside their Washington D.C. offices. The state of Alaska, via a letter drafted by Augie and signed by Governor Egan, submitted an official request to COMSAT for a satellite demonstration.

The satellite needed for the demonstration had not even been launched when the idea was conceived. The COMSAT Domestic Satellite application was pending before the FCC and launch of Intelsat IV was scheduled for later in the fall of 1971. Intelsat IV, the latest and largest commercial spacecraft at the time, would provide full service to many points in the Pacific area, and it could "see" Alaska. A unique feature of Intelsat IV was a steerable "spot beam" capable of focusing on an area such as Alaska.

As chairman of the Governor's Telecommunications Advisory Committee, Augie supervised the demonstration project. Bill Miller represented COMSAT, while Chuck Buck represented the state in his capacity as the governor's communications officer. The initial schedule for the demonstration at six Alaska villages in late 1971 was delayed until the spring and summer of 1972. RCA opposed the entire project and was responsible for its postponement. Although the project was open and RCA was invited and encouraged to participate, they (probably rightfully so) feared that COMSAT would become dominant and RCA would be aced out of the domestic satellite program. Remember as well that RCA had only months prior finalized their contract as the communications carrier for Alaska.

The demonstration of the sixteen-foot dish required special temporary authority from the FCC because they were prohibiting use of the dish for fear that such installations might be bothered by interference problems. But a demonstration is only a test, an examination of progress to determine future criteria. The state came on strong with the FCC, and RCA was overridden in their contest.

The May 4, 1972, Southeast Alaska Empire special news report captured the moment for all Alaskans:

> A television signal traveling 45,000 miles at the speed of light brought Juneau its first taste of space-age communications last night. An hour's television broadcast from Anchorage to Juneau via satellite went off without a hitch. It was the opening segment of a demonstration designed to show that existing satellite technology can overcome the communications problems posed by Alaska's vast and rugged expanses.

The satellite demonstration was a giant step forward in furtherance of long-term quality and comprehensive communications for Alaskans. A great deal of information was gained by the cooperative conduct of the operation. COMSAT representatives and engineers, RCA representatives, and state representatives oversaw the two-month testing procedure from Juneau to Kodiak, Bethel to Nome, Barrow to Fort Yukon— three days at each location with two-week intervals for disassembling, transporting, and testing. Transportation services were courtesy of the Air National Guard. The test results were significant to future licensing and disposition of telecommunications for Alaska. At the Fort Yukon demonstration site a special technical team from the Geophysical Institute, University of Alaska, maintained an extended study of satellite transmission and ionospheric phenomena in this far northern area.

The project was the first domestic satellite demonstration, with ramifications that transcended the transport of an earth station to six locations in Alaska. COMSAT's objectives were fulfilled; they not only determined the feasibility of using small aperture earth stations for communications in remote areas, but they assessed the operation of small terminals under conditions in high northern latitudes. They concluded that satellite acquisition, logistics, and ionospheric conditions provided no barriers to high quality video reception and two-way voice communications to a sixteen-foot terminal typical of those that might be used in remote areas.

RCA's participation in the project was to coordinate the terrestrial link of the demonstration. Integration of the terrestrial systems with satellite systems was critical for practical application of telecommunications in Alaska. The RCA Toll Center in Anchorage and their microwave facility links at Scotty Lake and 12-Mile (Hatcher Pass) were vital in transmitting programs originating in Anchorage to be beamed via satellite to the village receiver stations. As the expanding markets became readily apparent, RCA became an amenable and active participant in the small aperture earth station concept. Their proliferation of these systems throughout the state is no secret to today's "Touchtone" culture. In 1973 RCA acquired the COMSAT Bartlett Earth Station. The "wounds" sustained by RCA (Alascom) from Augie's opposition to their original plan had healed.

Those who have worked with Augie marvel at his willingness to work on behalf of the industry as a whole and for Alaska, rather than for the sole benefit of his own business. He is motivated not by profits nor by short-term benefits but by what the future might hold. He perceives clearly the need to know about Alaska (and its resources) if there is to be a future for her residents. This translates into a slow growth, long-term process.

Radio and television are an integral part of the education of people in Alaska. The electronic media influences people's understanding and attitudes and provides them with information on which to make decisions. There is more to broadcasting than making a buck. During Dr. William R. Wood's tenure as president of the University of Alaska, Augie helped formulate a proposal for a university radio station. The presentation to the Regent Board described the station as a laboratory for learning in the field. In addition, the station would provide a comprehensive, cross-cultural curriculum with extended educational opportunities in speech, journalism, business management, engineering, and others.

For these reasons, Augie has been an active supporter of public broadcasting, though many have questioned his sanity since public broadcasting is a competitor of commercial operations. Augie knows that public broadcasting offers additional broadcast opportunities to the people in Alaska, but he is also the first to criticize when public broadcasting strays from its intended purpose, especially in commercialization.

May 11, 1973, was a day of indescribable pride and exhilaration for Augie and his family. On that day he was presented an honorary degree of Doctor of Public Service by the University of Alaska. (The original citation is included in the Appendix.)

What Augie has done and continues to accomplish is the product of a self-made man, destined and determined by his own course. He has never taken for granted the precious opportunity to obtain a higher education. For him it was not to be, though that lack was not a barrier but a challenge to achieve that much more. His rewards now lie in the nurturing of others to personal and professional enrichment.

In August 1973, NTV threw one of the biggest promotions Anchorage had ever seen. There was cause to celebrate; not only was KTVA entering its twentieth year, but the longest running series, "Gunsmoke," was also commemorating its twentieth birthday. Who better to share in the festivities than "Miss Kitty" (Amanda Blake) and "Newly O'Brien" (Buck Taylor) of "Gunsmoke" fame. Both stars and their spouses participated in a week long itinerary of parties and sightseeing between Anchorage, Fairbanks, McKinley Park, and Valdez. For Pat and Augie the memories and the friendships have remained vivid.

If one year in the decade were to be singled out as having special significance, it would be 1974. Alaska radio history was made on February 2, 1974. The first full-time live network programming was brought to KFRB-AM, Fairbanks, and Anchorage stations KBYR-AM and KNIK-FM, all stations in the NTV family. It was a day for which Augie had worked and dreamed for thirty-five years. The radio service, by contract with RCA Alascom via satellite through the Bartlett Earth Station, would provide live news and sports, as well as other network broadcasts.

Another event early that year must have excited Augie. The March 18-24 Nielsen ratings showed that CBS had captured all ten of the top ten shows in the nation— unprecedented. CBS was hot!

On May 30, 1974, Augie witnessed NASA's launch of ATS-6, the world's most powerful communications satellite.

An electrifying event within itself, it was only one in a series of events that would impact the future of telecommunications in Alaska with regard to satellite utilization. The reason Augie was at the launch was a product of one of those wild and wonderful quirks of fate. He happened to be in Washington, D.C. on his annual east coast business junket. Fairchild Industries had invited Senator Ted Stevens and his staff assistant Hilary Hilscher to Cape Canaveral to watch the launch, and Senator Stevens invited Augie to accompany them. Fairchild Industries was the architect of the new breed ATS-F series of communications satellites, and Augie's old friend Dr. Werhner Von Braun was their vice-president of Engineering and Development as of July 1972.

Augie's sleepless nights and fantasies about the use of satellites in Alaska—not only for live television but also for remote emergency distress signaling, military surveillance, tsunami warning, weather, health and social services, and education in bush areas—were beginning to come true. Augie and Dr. Von Braun shared in these dreams; it was a unique relationship. What good is a communications satellite high above if it isn't put to use? For those two men there were no limits to what could be done.

Augie sat next to Dr. Von Braun on Fairchild's flight to the launch. He took the opportunity to suggest to Von Braun that he come back to Alaska for some fishing and hunting, as well as to see what communication advances had been made since his last visit. Dr. Von Braun, whose dreams of returning had never faded, was interested, as were others in the Fairchild hierarchy. The ATS-6 was serviceable to Alaska and the opportunity to promote its use would be politically and financially advantageous to their company. The people of Alaska would be the beneficiary!

Dr. Von Braun's trip to Alaska in September 1974 was again memorable for all concerned. His direction and inspiration provided support to Augie's persistent educational campaign in furtherance of satellite capabilities for Alaska. Von Braun's itinerary was again filled not only with business, but also with the pleasure of a two-day fishing trip to Lake Clark. One of the highlights of his trip was his spontaneous decision to obtain his float plane pilot certification, one of the few he was lacking. At Big Lake, with the Hiebert cabin and dock as the training base, he was successful in qualifying, with Augie, Pat, Cathy Jo, and Terry his passengers/flight crew.

At a banquet in Anchorage, sponsored by the Alaska chapter of the Association of the U. S. Army, Dr. Von Braun detailed the capabilities and opportunities of the new generation of communications satellites, especially the newly launched ATS-6. It was an impassioned speech, as was his manner, with emphasis on the position of Alaska within satellite communications. The gravity of his statement brought down to earth, so to speak, the communications potential within ATS-6 technology. Its high power and beaming capabilities would provide live television into low-cost receivers with the influence of a small and simple umbrella-like antenna. Heretofore, what "live via satellite" meant was the presence of large and costly ground station transmitters and receivers to direct a satellite signal to a TV set in the home.

The concept of live television direct to a simple receiver was brought home when Von Braun watched from Tanana as a doctor from the Native Service Hospital in Anchorage examined a young girl's broken thumb in Galena from a television screen. This diagnosis was accomplished through signals from ATS-6.

Dr. Von Braun also gave an impromptu lecture on satellites to the first-grade class in a small Yukon River village. Von Braun filled the classroom blackboard with detailed illustrations of satellites and earth stations while the children watched and listened with enraptured attention. All were mesmerized by his depth and power, his brilliance. As a teacher Von Braun excelled in his ability to make complex matters simple, thereby heightening the comprehension level for everyone.

At the end of the lecture, a youngster asked, "I understand, but what can we do with this? Dr. Von Braun responded, "What do you want to do with it?" From then on, satellite technology was viewed with that perspective. The doors of the imagination were flung open. Augie relished that moment, a moment he had been grooming for so long.

• • •

During the spring and summer of 1974 a monumental undertaking was begun. And it all started with "Captain Kangaroo." Because PBS programming offered little entertainment for village viewing, Bob Arnold, executive director of AEBC, asked Augie to tape some of the more popular CBS shows and send them for viewing in the Mini-TV villages. It was thought to be a simple request, but as Don Clancy of CBS relates, "Augie has always been dedicated to the rule of Law. A man's work, his music, his book, his scripts, his performances, should be protected against piracy and outright stealing. Augie viewed the Copyright Act, as did CBS, to protect copyright owners against the theft of their performance without payment." Don Clancy, along with CBS copyright expert Harry Olsson, joined with Augie in a series of meetings to find a way to legally provide television programs to the bush.

Authorization for the rebroadcast of "Captain Kangaroo" was based on the fact that a translator for which Mini-TV stations were licensed, were by definition an extension of an affiliate station; therefore the authorization was by Translator Agreement, with a Special Temporary Authority granted by the FCC.

The success of the Mini-TV tape project was an inspiration to Augie. The construction of the Trans-Alaska Oil Pipeline, with its numerous workers' camps, was underway in 1974. The pipeline was situated, for the most part, in the middle of nowhere, but that "nowhere" had a population of twenty-two thousand construction workers. It was a perfect setting for the infant Mini-TV concept, as Ted Lehne, NTV Fairbanks station manager, counseled Augie. Therefore, along with his efforts to procure authorization to distribute "Captain Kangaroo" to Mini-TV villages, Augie submitted proposals to develop a Mini-TV system along the Trans-Alaska Pipeline from Valdez to Prudhoe Bay. The system would utilize taped network programming as a source of news, sports, and entertainment for pipeline workers. The negotiations were complicated and involved important safeguards to insure copyright integrity, but with the cooperation of the CBS Television Network, Augie received authorization to provide programming to all the camps.

Mini-TV stations were established by the end of 1974 at all eighteen construction camps, as well as the terminal camp at Valdez. Four additional stations were later installed and all were operational during the peak construction period until 1976.

The beauty of the Mini-TV system was in its transmission. A Mini-TV transmission of a conventional tape could be picked up by a typical antenna system for individual TV set use. A construction worker, away from home for weeks on end, working many hours a day, seven days a week, could bring along a TV set and feel "more at home." Perhaps it served to diminish some stress-related reactions as well, such as the incident at the Churchill Camp in remote Canada where a group of workers demolished the entire facility with their bulldozers.

Augie recounts the procedures used to implement this incredible project when the pipeline construction began in the spring of 1974. He also fine tunes the issue of copyright integrity in the following:

> I began negotiating with the FCC to determine whether the authority granted to the AEBC for three pubic Mini-TV stations might also be applicable to tape delayed network programming of entertainment, sports and news provided to pipeline workers. The FCC agreed.
>
> It was also necessary to convince the CBS Television Network that this would not cause disastrous problems. The potential liability to the network was enormous. CBS had nothing to gain, because the entire Alaskan population was such a small part of its circulation universe that it meant nothing to CBS's bottom line. On the other hand, the network contracts with TV programming suppliers for millions of dollars worth of programming rights annually, and an abuse of those rights could create an enormous liability. Typical abuses would be to illegally tape record programming and sell it (for example, to Saudi Arabia for entertainment in their oil field camps) or to play back the tapes an unauthorized second time on the Mini-TV station.
>
> Network/programming contracts typically call for two runs—the original network release, and one rerun. A second, or unauthorized rerun would breach the contract and subject

the network to suit and damages. Finally, through the genius of Mr. Don Clancy, CBS Network vice-president of contracts and legal services, it was determined that the network could protect itself so long as the affiliated station did the taping and made the tapes available to Alyeska Pipeline authorities, which properly logged and identified the programs and returned the tapes to the affiliate for erasing after play at the Alyeska camps. The responsibility for this method of control was the affiliate's, and the network would be in compliance with their program suppliers and their contracts with the network.

The center of distribution to the Alyeska pipeline was Fairbanks. My company, Northern Television, Inc., owns and operates KTVF there, with a primary CBS network affiliation. Midnight Sun Broadcasting then owned and operated KFAR-TV, with a primary NBC network affiliation. KTVF and KFAR-TV both shared ABC network programming through a "per program" affiliation agreement because no third station existed in Fairbanks. Northern TV applied to the FCC for eighteen Mini-TV licenses along the pipeline route, and shared this application data with Midnight Sun Broadcasting which requested identical Mini-TV licenses from the FCC. These applications were necessary to comply with the delicate network legal requirement that network programming could be used on a Translator/Mini-TV station only "as an extension of their affiliated station agreement."

The FCC subsequently granted identical Mini-TV licenses to both KTVF and KFAR-TV to serve all the camps, but with a unique twist to satisfy FCC legal requirements. It authorized different Mini-TV call letters to the KTVF licenses than to the KFAR-TV licenses! Technically, when a camp Mini-TV station transmitted a CBS network program at a camp, the KTVF mini call letter applied; when an NBC program was aired, the KFAR-TV Mini-TV call letter applied. This unique system provided programming to the pipeline camps until 1976, when it was no longer needed. To provide the service, KFAR-TV and KTVF had to make as many program tape copies as there were Mini-TV stations operating in the camps, because Alyeska had an airlift distribution daily to the entire pipeline system out of Fairbanks and did not want to bicycle programming from one camp to another."

Augie's original commitment for television as an option for recreation and as a viable conduit for public service programming contributed to his pursuit of the project. Additional taped programming from other sources such as the University of Alaska were televised in the camps as well. Programs such as "Tax Preparation Tips" and a "Log Cabin Builders Course" were seen. But news and sports were probably the programs that brought civilization closest to the tundra. There is something about a football game that can be denied no man!

In January 1975 the FCC also granted licenses to KBYR and KFRB to construct and operate low power (50-watt) transmitters at eighteen construction camps to deliver radio programming along the pipeline. However, with the exception of the North Slope/Prudhoe Bay Base Camp, none of the radio transmission facilities hit the airwaves, a product of insufficient circuitry along the pipeline. Telemetry for radio was superseded by telephone line overload. The "morale phone" in each camp meant a great deal to workers distanced for long periods from family and friends.

In an effort to salvage one radio location, Augie and George Howard, NTV chief engineer in Anchorage, took a trip to Prudhoe Bay on March 25, 1975, to test a 50-watt transmitter with two different types of antennas. For three days they experimented at 25 degrees below zero in 25-knot winds (the wind chill was 75 below!). They experienced much interference because they couldn't get a ground in the frozen tundra. A neutral wire used as an artificial ground proved fruitless as well; there were too many nearby power lines. So AM radio was doomed for the North Slope.

FM, on the other hand, is not subject to "noise" nor is a ground necessary. Low power FM is capable of successful transmission above and beyond competing static. The solution was simple, but the resolution would be a challenge with the FCC. Atlantic Richfield supported an FM station in their permission and funding of equipment if Augie would acquire the necessary licenses.

"Things are different in Alaska" rang again through the hallowed halls of the FCC when Augie requested a number of waivers to his license for the Prudhoe Bay radio project. First, permission was needed for an FM translator to rebroadcast an AM station, KBYR in Anchorage. (This had never been allowed.) Second, since the stations were eight hundred miles apart, rebroadcast could not be off-the-air;

therefore the signal needed to be by satellite. Third, the initial 10-watt operation coverage was found to be inadequate for the expanded base camp. There was a need to upgrade to a 100-watt unit. Putting the whole scheme into perspective, the landmark result was the first 100-watt FM translator, rebroadcasting an AM station, not off-the-air.

The entire pipeline communications concept was celebrated for its innovation. Alaska watched with great interest as the Mini-TV network developed and progressed into a successful story of providing TV programming to remote areas of Alaska.

As one event begets another in telecommunications, so another major event occurred in late 1975 when the state called Anchorage broadcasters together. The governor's Office of Telecommunications assigned them, along with a legislative contingent, the task of researching a system of distributing programming from Anchorage network-affiliated stations to twenty-three remote Alaska community Mini-TV stations via satellite. It was called the TV Demonstration Project (TVDP). George Shaginaw, deputy director of the governor's Office of Telecommunications, was appointed the state's principal representative to interface with broadcasters. Augie had recently worked with the CBS network and the FCC on network affiliate programming, distribution, and copyright issues and licensing. So Augie took the lead along with Shaginaw in approaching the networks about the project. The local affiliate committee consisted of Duane Triplett and Dick Zook (ABC) and Al Bramstedt, Sr. and Charlie Gray (NBC).

All of 1976 was used to investigate and fine tune the Demonstration Project concept with the FCC and to negotiate with the networks. With a $1.5 million legislative appropriation confirmed, the state decided to target TVDP start-up for January 15, 1977.

The project called for the state's lease of a year of one full-time satellite transponder from Alascom at $500,000; the installation of receivers and transmitters for twenty-three villages at $20,000 for each village station. (Diomede Island, a twenty-fourth site was dropped from the test because the earth station could not "see" the satellite.) Programs, delay center, and management consumed the balance of the $1.5 million. The twenty-four initial village sites were: Ambler, Anaktuvuk Pass, Gambell, King Cove, Kipnuk, Mekoryuk, Noatak, St. Paul, Savoonga, Shungnak, Tenakee Springs, Cape Pole, Chitina, Diomede, Emmonak, Holy Cross, Larsen Bay, Nulato, Old Harbor, Perryville, Pilot Point, Point Hope, Shageluk, and Tatitlek.

The week leading up to the January 15 start-up date was a flurry of activity, as reflected by Augie's account of the last-minute hurdles that had to be overcome:

> Not all of the three New York network management officials thoroughly understood the concept. Therefore, I volunteered to represent the Anchorage network-affiliated stations, and Mr. Shaginaw and I traveled to New York the first week in January to attend meetings and obtain concurrences from all of the networks. After calls on their respective legal and affiliate relations officials, the networks authorized TVDP, with the understanding that it was a test demonstration, and if any abuses occurred potentially detrimental to the network, the agreement would be canceled and the test terminated immediately. Mr. Shaginaw and I promised to return in one year with a report, at which time the networks would decide if the concept could be implemented on a continuing basis.

In the meantime, the state Office of Telecommunications had applied to the FCC for twenty-three of the twenty-four remote village sites to be part of the TVDP, but the FCC had not acted on them, although the system was scheduled to go on line January 15.

Mr. Shaginaw had to return to Juneau from New York, but I proceeded on to Washington, D.C. to work with the state legal counsel at the time, and made contact with the director of the Translator Division at the FCC, Gordon Oppenheimer. As it turned out, not only were the Mini-TV licenses not granted, some had not even begun to be processed, and one or two were still in the FCC "in basket." This was the Thursday before the scheduled Monday beginning of the TVDP! Credit Mr. Oppenheimer with being a most unusual and understanding bureaucratic regulator. He told us that if we guaranteed there would be no abuse of the system he would authorize the state by telegram the next day, Friday, and the necessary paperwork would follow as he had time to process it. TVDP thus began on schedule."

(During this hectic time, Augie somehow managed to welcome into the world his second grandchild, Melissa Ann-Marie.)

Management of this new satellite delivery system was established under the auspices of the Rural Alaska Television Network (RATNET). A RATNET Advisory Council was also formed. Augie elaborates on the significance of this satellite project:

In retrospect, I don't believe anyone would deny that the RATNET system was about as unique and unusual as anything ever conceived for service to both remote and urban areas throughout the vastness of Alaska. Satellite delivery made it possible, and it was and still is costly. However, to maximize use of the satellite transponder made available by Alascom, some very innovative technical developments were implemented. . . . A system that had all the potential for disagreements, impossible scheduling and disaster worked just fine. RATNET communities, through choice by their own committee representatives received virtually everything they wanted, and urban communities throughout the State received virtually all the live news and sports programming they desired. RATNET was and is a classic example of dedicated people working together to achieve a highly desirable goal.

This marvelous system became a model of interest to several foreign countries. Australian and Chinese representatives inspected it, and Augie escorted and introduced around a technical delegation from South Africa, who were recommended to him by CBS. Their view was that RATNET was a fantastic and highly successful concept.

The TVDP was not immune from controversy. Local commercial broadcasters were skeptical about the longevity of the program. As a one-year "demonstration" at the mercy of legislative funding, they felt it was tenuous at best. Their fears were expressed as a double jeopardy—in permitting their urban viewers to enjoy the benefits of live sports and news, even on a limited basis, they might be caught with the bill to sustain it at the termination of the project.

Many felt the system, seen as a temporary effort to provide television service to the bush, would harm more than help rural Alaskans. Could the project be maintained by funding? Should the state be the custodian of the system indefinitely? Would an undue burden be placed on the rural native Alaskan social fabric?

The project was unprecedented. It was innovative and technologically progressive, and it served the purpose for which communications satellites were invented—for Alaska (according to Augie). Yes, there were risks, but those are to be expected when the course is based on what is right rather than expedient. The key to success is to remain steadfast and not succumb to criticism. Rural Alaska had the right to access.

The first year of the TVDP was a·success, as Augie explains:

> The TVDP turned out to be so successful and popular a project in the rural communities served, that the legislature provided continuing funds, and Mr. Shaginaw and I returned to visit all three TV networks in New York in January 1978 to make our promised report. They were pleased with what they heard, and signed off on the whole concept as an acceptable continuing operation, but with the same admonition that if any abuse or deviation from the agreement occurred, they could terminate authority to their Anchorage affiliated stations at any time.

The number of Mini-TV sites grew, as each year additional funding added new locations to the system. As time went on the project became more cost effective. Many villages were integrated with Alascom's two-way voice communications, an upgrade in Alaska's telephone system, and therefore it was necessary only to retrofit what was in place with a TV receiver.

Alascom had installed earth stations in many villages for telephone service prior to the TVDP. During the winter, as snow piled up on the satellite dishes, the transmission noise increased, and telephone usage declined, as did revenues to Alascom. The snow levels were never reported to Alascom so that appropriate action could be taken. When television arrived, however, and villagers discovered that a snow load on the dish meant no picture, the entire maintenance problem was resolved.

In bringing rural villages on line for television, the state decided to introduce some villages to educational TV first (as opposed to entertainment TV). Some villages might then have only educational TV, while a neighboring village might have a channel choice. In Huslia, where there was no option, some innovative villagers discovered they could breach security locks at the earth station building, change the frequency of the downlink, and have exclusive entertainment television. Alascom then had to fly in, restore the original frequency, and make security repairs and improvements. This happened over and over again. But on one such trip, Alascom technicians were "welcomed" off the plane by three Huslians; two of them were carrying shotguns (and it wasn't duck hunting season!) They informed Alascom that the earth station was just fine and they should get back on the plane and go home . . . which they did.

This incident highlights the intensity of the struggle to maintain balance between entertainment and education in programming for rural television. In 1980 the state legislature decided to fund an additional transponder for exclusive education and instruction. It was called LearnAlaska. Instructional TV therefore had its own channel and the RATNET channel brought entertainment, including daytime soap operas and game shows.

LearnAlaska was managed by the state Department of Education and the University of Alaska. It was begun to enhance academic opportunities to rural areas of Alaska where educational experiences in small school districts are limited and need of assistance to maintain certain course offerings to fulfill state mandated requirements.

LearnAlaska provided live and locally produced broadcasts, as well as taped history, nature, and nationally produced health shows. In addition to a school curriculum course menu, LearnAlaska also offered state-wide audio-conferencing, telecourses for credit, and live coverage of Native Alaskan events such as the Festival of Native Arts, Indian-Eskimo Olympics, and the Alaska Federation of Native Conventions.

(Regrettably, LearnAlaska was dealt a fatal blow in 1986 when the legislature removed funding for the satellite time and equipment for the 250 rural villages served.)

For a while sociologists objected to advertising in the programming. They contended that the commercials were destructive to the native culture. But others, including Augie, argued that commercials provided the positive service of a shopping guide. Urban dwellers have their own methods of consumer education, with miles of malls for comparative shopping. Rural people have learned from commercials how to more responsibly make their purchases, mostly through catalog or other rural distribution outlets and primarily in bulk order.

The ultimate success of RATNET is determined by those served by it—their evaluation of the benefits television has introduced to rural Alaska and the village communities.

When a native woman, herself a successful businesswoman, school board member, and mother of four young children, was told that RATNET was in jeopardy of dissolution, she responded with tears, dejection, incredulity, and fist-on-the-table fury. The family supper, she explained, is scheduled to coincide with the national newscast. Her ten-year-old daughter, now acutely aware of the world around her because of this exposure, submits her questions and comments about current events. This vital opportunity is one the mother herself was denied in her growing up years, and she does not want it denied to her children. The scene is moving; the drama is real. It is a vindication of Augie's philosophy and commitment to provide telecommunication facilities to all Alaskans.

It has been said that the state has no right or business to conglomerate and control telecommunications by legislative mandate and financial support. If there were another way, it would be done. From a practical point of view, the system has to be a state function, a more economically feasible proposition than cable or commercial management. Alaska is unique; what works well is supported by rewards beyond the obvious. Do we not all pay for our own quality of life? RATNET probably benefits a greater number of Alaskans than any other program in state government. As opposed to no system at all, it is a wise expenditure of state money with obvious trade-offs.

Augie's bottom line in assessing the state television delivery system is "don't mess with success." And that was the gist of an extensive response he prepared to a discussion draft titled, "A Report to the Alaska Legislature in Response to Intent Language Regarding Telecommunications in the FY88 Budget," when during the 1988 session the legislature was devising alternatives in an effort to meet budgetary limitations.

(The rural/urban dichotomy was painfully revealed in a newspaper article published in the *Anchorage Daily News* and reproduced in the Appendix.)

• • •

Augie Hiebert is a man compelled to rise to a challenge, and the seed of the biggest challenge of them all was planted in late 1977. In September, Alaskans for Better Media (ABM) allied with Media Access Project, a Washington D.C. firm, to protest the proposed sale of Midnight Sun Broadcasting, Inc. (ABM was a coalition consisting of Alaska Chapter Sierra Club, Alaska Center for the Environment, Sitka Conservation Society, Tongass Conservation Society, Fairbanks Chapter Friends of the Earth, Trustees for Alaska, Anchorage Women's Resource Center, Anchorage Native Caucus, and Alaska Public Interest Research Group.)

Although TV and radio operations are private enterprises, they are regulated by the Federal Communications Commission. ABM threatened to block the sale and approval of transfer by the FCC if Midnight Sun did not meet their demands. The basis for the demands was a study ABM had allegedly conducted of local station FCC renewal applications. The core of ABM's demands related to minority hiring, public affairs programming, and requests of $7,500 from each station as reimbursement for their research and as seed money to set up a local office and staff.

The assertions of alleged impropriety came at a time when the D-2 lands issue was in the heat of its publicity wild fire. The D-2 lands issue was a section of federal legislation designed to identify what remaining federal lands should be set aside for parks and wilderness, and what areas should be left open for mining, oil exploration, and so on. The assertions also came on the shirt-tails of similar accusations and subsequent settlement with stations in Wyoming. Alaska and Wyoming evidently were the only remaining states deficient in citizen advisory groups—another focus of ABM.

By mid-December 1977, ABM's demands as well as the public's reaction to them were well publicized. The *Anchorage Times* was especially noteworthy in its coverage. Bob Atwood, editor of the *Times*, was supportive of the broadcasters because he saw a takeover threat to the broadcast media in the state by a special interest group that was counterproductive to Alaska's economic growth and development. "Letters to the Editor" cited objections to ABM principles and reflected a sense of outrage at their denigration of Alaskan broadcasters.

On December 19, 1977, Augie went on the air to deliver an impassioned editorial defending the rights of his longtime friend and competitor, Alvin O. (Bram) Bramstedt, Sr., to sell his stations in Alaska. Augie's aversion to the blackmail tactics of ABM toward Alaskan broadcasters was the primary motivation for his comments, and his concern for Bram's failing health further fueled the fire. But the bottom line was that regardless of Bram's health, he had the right to sell his company. Perhaps Augie's rare appearance on camera was intended to boost morale in the midst of a confusing and uncertain media campaign by what was ascertained to be a group of non-Alaskans calling itself Alaskans for Better Media. (The text of Augie's public appeal is reprinted in the Appendix in its entirety.)

The next several days saw a flurry of activities and comments. On December 20, 1977, a citizen's group was organized to support renewal of local broadcast stations. The group called itself Alaskans in Support of Alaskan Broadcasting. Two days later, Senator Stevens charged ABM with "extortion" for its cash demands. He also questioned if ABM was acting in retaliation against local broadcasters because of their involvement in discussing public issues such as D-2 land legislation. On December 23, the president of the Cook Inlet Native Association announced that the association was dropping its affiliation with the Anchorage Native Caucus which was in alliance with ABM. On the following day there were more public comments opposing ABM principles and tactics and supporting local broadcasters.

In January 1978, NTV performed an unprecedented service. Augie organized a citizen's advisory group composed of a cross-section of social, economic, cultural, and religious representatives. In March, ABM responded to this affirmative action by NTV by filing three petitions with the FCC against Midnight Sun, Northern Television, and Central Alaska (KIMO-TV et al.) to deny renewal of their respective licenses.

On July 19, 1978, Midnight Sun withdrew its request for transfer of ownership. ABM then began to force the issue of a hearing. Augie reacted to these developments in an article in the *Anchorage Times* on August 29: "I would rather go bankrupt. If it costs $1 million to go to a hearing, I'll go broke. But I'll leave the country in a barrel before I'll give up the responsibility of my station."

On July 17, 1979, nearly a year after Midnight Sun withdrew its request to sell its stations, Midnight Sun and ABM settled. Midnight Sun, with its back against the wall and facing a costly hearing, succumbed to ABM's demands. Midnight Sun paid ABM $30,000 to withdraw its petition against license renewal and the sale of Midnight Sun properties, plus pledged free air time to ABM to espouse its various causes. Had ABM's petition against Midnight Sun (or any company) been designated for a full FCC hearing, the costs would have been at least $500,000 and delays up to ten years. Since Al Bramstedt was not well and wanted to sell and be relieved of management, he had little alternative but to cave in to ABM's demands. (A midwestern TV station had an identical suit filed against it by the same Washington, D.C., law firm behind ABM; that suit cost ten million dollars and took almost eleven years to settle.)

On December 5, 1979, NTV suffered a significant setback. The FCC voted to permit ABM access to NTV's confidential financial statements. Defense costs for NTV to this point already tallied around $100,000. More importantly, the allegations by the special interest consortium were an affront to Augie's integrity as a man and as a broadcaster.

Unfortunately, the seven year, $400,000 nightmare would continue into the next decade.

COMSAT sixteen-foot satellite dish test demonstration earth station at Nome Site, Front Street, June 9, 1972. Note compactness of technical equipment housing at left.

Earth Station at Nome Site overlooking the Bering Sea.

Intricacy of Earth Station technical equipment, transistorized and mobile.

Dr. Augie Hiebert! May 11, 1973, Honorary doctoral degree in
Public Service, University of Alaska.

KFRB Fairbanks celebration of first full-time live network satellite radio broadcast service in Alaska, February 2, 1974. Ted Lehne, NTV Fairbanks general manager with Augie and photo of Alascom's Bartlett Earth Station.

KBYR Anchorage celebration of live network radio service, February 2, 1974. Steve Heller, Alascom with Ron Moore, Anchorage NTV general manager at KBYR Control.

Photo by Augie Hiebert

Cape Canaveral ATS-6 satellite rocket blast off, May 30, 1974.

Photo by Augie Hiebert

Dr. Wernher Von Braun taking a break from his float plane certification flights on Big Lake, September 1974.

Dr. Von Braun's Hiebert flight crew, (from left) Pat Hiebert, Terry Hiebert, Pilot Von Braun, Cathy Hiebert, and Augie, Big Lake, September 1974.

A typical village earth station. From Alascom, described by Alascom's Tom Jenson: "On the left of the photo, the upright cabinet contains Alascom's long distance switching equipment. In the foreground on the left wall, the two lower units are Alascom's television downlinking modules (one for educational TV and the other for entertainment TV). The two upper units are the world-famous 10 watt mini-TV transmitters, owned by the state of Alaska, one for educational TV and the other for entertainment. More than three hundred locations throughout Alaska have the same type facilities in place for television programming."

CHAPTER 6

THE THRILL
OF VICTORY:
THE 1980s

T he same dark cloud that hung heavy over the late 1970s continued to blanket the first four years of the new decade, but through it shone an occasional sunbeam. As relentless as was Alaskans for Better Media, so too was Augie. By now he was alone in his fight. No other broadcaster could or would stand up to the challenge; the fiscal commitment was too high a price to pay. They knew it, Augie knew it. And in the end, his peers would be among the first to applaud his singular effort.

In the early 1980s Augie's rewards were many for projects he continued to pursue in his labors of love for broadcasting and Alaska. Again, he "lighted many lights rather than curse the darkness."

The end of July 1980, Augie and Hank Hove, president of NTV Fairbanks, met with all seven FCC commissioners in Washington, D.C. The meeting was on behalf of the Alaska Broadcasters Association (ABA), of which Hank was president, and was the highlight of Hank's and Augie's broadcasting careers.

Hank and Augie presented to the FCC three topics of imminent concern to Alaska broadcasters. These issues were not resolved right away, and they became the major focus of an intensive campaign in the early 1980s. In the order of priority, those topics were:

1. The dangers of the FCC deregulating network programming protection which prohibits local cable systems from importing network signals for simultaneous release where there is a network affiliate. This was critical to every commercial TV station in Alaska operating on a programming tape-delay basis.

2. The subject of Arctic propagation and the proposal to provide a study by the University of Alaska/Geophysical Institute so the FCC could develop new Clear Channel 1-A Skywave curves. This affects nearly every commercial and public radio station in Alaska.

3. The recommendation to move the FCC monitoring station to a new site outside of Anchorage proper. This affects every Anchorage broadcast station—AM, FM, TV—as well as amateur radio operators.

On July 20, 1980, the FCC had deregulated the cable industry. Alaska's network-affiliated broadcasters, as off-shore stations not contiguous to the Lower 48, were subject to tape delays in programming from one week to three weeks. The networks had not yet entered the satellite era for service to Alaska and Hawaii. Under deregulation cable could air network programming first and everything that followed on network-affiliated stations would be "reruns." Once the networks began to serve Alaska and Hawaii via satellite (and this was inevitable), the problem would be resolved. What the Alaska Broadcasters Association sought was a temporary "Alaska-Hawaii Waiver." Hank and Augie argued that rules applied to the industry as a whole would have a devastating effect on TV stations not having the advantage of full network interconnection.

The Clear Channel and FCC Monitoring Station issues were separate, but not mutually exclusive. Both problems, unique to Alaska, were preventing radio stations from upgrading their power output to serve a rapidly growing metropolitan area.

The meeting Augie and Hank had with the FCC had a powerful impact. It was the genesis for Augie's development of "Alaska Day at the FCC" a year later. Augie resolved, "If we can't take the Commission to Alaska, we'll take Alaska to the Commission." On September 28, 1981, Augie arranged, through the ABA, a comprehensive and entertaining "trip through Alaska."

A contingency of Alaskan broadcasters met with the seven FCC commissioners during the morning session, while the afternoon was spent with key staff members from the Field and Broadcast Bureaus. Informal and formal discussions throughout the day, along with a taste of Alaska at a dinner buffet at the Metropolitan Club, provided a forum to explain Alaskan problems and Alaskan conditions that rate special Commission attention. Included in the event was a tape, narrated by Ruben Gaines. Talks were given by the following or their representative in attendance: ABA President Patty Harpel; Duane Triplett (KIMO-TV, Anchorage); Al Bramstedt, Jr. (KTUU-TV, Anchorage); Tom Busch (KNOM-radio, Nome); Gene Henderson (KYAK/KGOT-FM, Anchorage); Roy Robinson (KFQD, Anchorage); Major Bill Whipple (Air Force Arctic Broadcasting Squadron); and Dr. Charles Northrip (executive director, Alaska Public Broadcasting Commission).

The occasion was memorable and effective. For Augie it was more than memorable. Because of the continuing ABM challenge against Northern Television license renewals, Augie and NTV representatives Ron Moore and Hank Hove, while in attendance, were not allowed to take part in the presentations. For every rose, there is a thorn; ABM was drawing blood.

But a rose, by any other name, is still a rose, and on March 30, 1981, KFRB radio in Fairbanks, a member of the NTV family since 1965, increased its power to 50,000 watts. In addition, since the call letters for stations KFAR and KFRB were close enough to cause confusion, a decision was made to change KFRB's call letters, along with increasing its area of coverage in Fairbanks. Commemorative of Augie's early radio days in Fairbanks, the station was renamed KCBF (the call letters came from his ham radio call K7CBF).

Augie worked constantly to improve the quality of his stations within a highly competitive and often restrictive market. His efforts produced many rewards; every hurdle became a historical milestone. The hurdles in Anchorage, however, have been higher and more of a millstone.

"I shot myself in the foot on that one," was Augie's response when queried with regard to the FCC Monitoring Station and his quest for increased power for KBYR. Augie had been in consort with the FCC Monitoring Station in Anchorage from its debut. Jim McKinney, Chief Mass Media Bureau, FCC, recounts in a letter (reproduced in its entirety in the Appendix) Augie's commitment to improve deficiencies in Alaskan communications and media access.

Augie was responsible, with the congressional backing of Senator Ted Stevens, for resuscitating the FCC Field Office and Monitoring Station in Anchorage. Between 1981 and 1983, federal funding for the Anchorage operations was declining; the Monitoring Station in Alaska was on the endangered species list. Augie's support of the Monitoring Station's continuance, however, conflicted with his desire to increase power for his radio station, KBYR. The Field Bureau has restrictive location requirements for a powerful radio station to prevent interference with their own monitoring operations. In spite of his desire to increase KBYR's power, Augie pursued maintaining the FCC Monitoring Station in Anchorage. In a letter to Lieutenant Governor Terry Miller, who was also chairman of the governor's Task Force on Telecommunications, Augie explains the motivation:

[The Monitoring Station's] service to the state and the country far outweighs the discomfort of broadcasters and other communications services receiving technical notices of violation.

The FCC Monitoring Station is in an essential position to triangulate with the Hawaiian FCC Monitoring Station to locate lost aircraft, and ships at sea not only in Alaska waters but in the North Pacific Ocean.

Further, they are in an extremely sensitive position to do surveillance monitoring of Asiatic and Siberian foreign transmissions which have obvious intelligence benefits to our country.

Several other broadcasters and I have made a strong appeal to Senators Stevens and Murkowski requesting continued funds to support the FCC Monitoring Station here.

The Monitoring Station survived the guillotine, but for Augie to increase his radio station's power output, he will have to find a new location for an AM tower. As simple as that task might seem, it has not been for Augie. No viable location has yet been found.

People of high integrity and Christian values are considered for nomination to exclusive membership in the Knights of Malta. Two hundred years of royal ancestry is a prerequisite for nomination in Europe, but not so in North America. On April 24, 1982, Augie was invested into the Sovereign Military Hospitaller Order of St. John of Jerusalem, of Rhodes and Malta, Southern Association in the United States.

Although the Order is humble in its identity, it is noble in its global mission. The Knights of Malta care for the sick and poor, and the Pope is Superior of the Order, whose history dates back to the Crusades in the eleventh century. The Crusaders during 1000 AD were dedicated to the defense of the Holy Land. Countries in Europe that subscribed to the Crusade pooled their resources to build a hospital in the Holy Land to care for wounded Crusaders and pilgrims. The hospital needed protection as well, which prompted the foundation of the Knights of St. John's Hospitallers.

When the Holy Land was captured by the Turks, the St. John's Hospitallers were ousted to the Island of Rhodes. Here they remained for four hundred years as the Knights of Rhodes, fulfilling their commission to build, maintain, and protect facilities for the sick and poor. When Rhodes too was seized by the Turks, the Knights fled by ship and reestablished on Malta where they built a hospital that is supported today by the Order's worldwide membership of ten thousand. On April 23, 1988, Augie was joined by Pat, who was invested into the Order of the Knights of Malta, as a Dame of Malta.

• • •

In 1982 Walter Cronkite retired as CBS news anchor. Augie had remained persistent in his bid to lure the veteran broadcaster to Alaska for a royal tour of the state. On June 7, 1982, Cronkite appeared as guest banquet speaker before a packed ABA Convention in Anchorage. Everyone enjoyed his visit and the enthusiasm and thirst for adventure that radiated from him.

Augie and Pat escorted Walter and his wife, Betsy, through the state, and as Walter touched Alaskans, so too he was touched by them. While Pat and Betsy flew commercial to Kotzebue, the National Guard ushered Walter and Augie to Kotzebue. Then it was off to the small Northwestern Alaska village of Selawik. As they deplaned from the Otter craft, they were greeted by a child's voice, "Hi, Walter!" Even at the ends of the earth, a child recognized him and called him by name.

The itinerary extended to Prudhoe Bay where Arco and Sohio gave him a red carpet greeting. Then it was on to Fairbanks, where his welcome was as cordial as the familiar warmth of the interior summer sun. In Fairbanks he was treated to a ride along the Chena River on the stern-wheeler "Discovery" and to the mesmerizing scenic beauty. This was followed by a celebration with a crowd of local people and NTV staff.

At the University of Alaska the tour continued through the many laboratories of Arctic research. The study of permafrost, significant to northern Alaskan construction, was demonstrated by a trip through an ice cave.

The Geophysical Institute Center of auroral study was of great interest to Mr. Cronkite. One of his upcoming "CBS Universe" programs was dedicated to the wonders of the Aurora. An account of the research at the Institute indicated to him that a part of his program needed to be revised. A quick phone call to New York corrected everything before the production was finished and aired.

In Augie's estimation, CBS News stories were not always forgiving in their portrayal of Alaska. Take, for instance, Terry Drinkwater's expose on the "Trashing of Alaska," reported in the early 1980s. The phone circuits were busy that day! The piece was hailed by Governor Jay Hammond, and the entire script was read into the Alaska legislative record. Augie did not respond to the story with the same vigor. His quest to elevate misconceptions of Alaska from igloo to the twentieth century were hard fought. "Look beyond the trash," he reaffirmed. "Look at the grandeur of Mt. McKinley!"

In late 1982 KBYR radio broadcast from the Arco Prudhoe Bay Camp station, an extension of the KBYR listening family. The remote broadcast was a natural. Most workers rotate on the North Slope one week on, with one week off; and many call Anchorage Bowl or the Matanuska Valley home. The idea of the remote was to expand the scope of KBYR's influence—to bring things closer to home and boost morale among the workers on the North Slope. In April 1988, the remote broadcast was repeated courtesy of Arco Alaska, only this time the broadcast originated from Prudhoe Bay and nearby Kuparuk. The community of Kuparuk is smaller than Prudhoe Bay, although the Kuparuk oil field is more extensive for long-range development and expansion. The two share in healthy competition.

Knowing this, Augie surreptitiously decided to make the broadcast a by-play contest—one against the other. Augie was the engineer at Kuparuk, with announcer Jan Andrews, while Ron Moore, Bob Dehne, and John Antonuk held down the fort at Prudhoe Bay. Once they were all installed, Augie told Jan, "We're going to play up the fact that our camp is the number one site." Announcers Andrews and Dehne made the most of the situation, and by the end of the remote broadcast, Kuparuk wanted its own radio station. "If you're serious, let me know," Augie told them. "I'm headed to Washington and we can work on the necessary waivers." One waiver was a little different this time; the area to be served was a large one, requiring 1000-watts of power. The licensing procedure was for 10, but there was no problem. Neighboring Eskimo villages would be served and had expressed an interest in supporting the proposition. Prudhoe Bay, at 100 watts, however, caught wind of Kuparuk's desire for a 1000-watt operation. The rest will be history!

For Pat and Augie the NTV thirtieth anniversary celebration on December 11, 1983, was a special highlight.

They were surprised not only to see many out-of-state friends and family, but also by the Alaska Broadcasters Association announcement of the annual "Augie Hiebert Scholarship Fund." The fund, administered by ABA and underwritten by NTV, was instituted to provide opportunities for young people wanting to enter the broadcast industry. A high school senior from Alaska is selected each year from among many applicants to receive a $1500 scholarship. Not only is aid given for the pursuit of academic goals, but NTV also extends to an "Augie Hiebert Scholar" the opportunity to apprentice in a professional broadcast career.

On January 3, 1984, Alaska celebrated the silver anniversary of its statehood, and Augie was recognized as one of several distinguished leaders in Alaska's effort to become the forty-ninth state. At the University of Alaska, Fairbanks, Augie served as Master of Ceremonies for the statewide live radio and TV simulcast of the documentary program in commemoration of the twenty-five years of statehood. The program, commissioned by Festival Fairbanks '84 of which Dr. William Wood was director, was by resolution of the Alaska legislature. Attending the event were "Founders for Alaska Statehood," including delegates to the Alaska Constitutional Convention held in 1955. The occasion is also remembered as one of former Governor William A. Egan's last public addresses, and probably his most superlative.

In September 1984, Dr. Sylvia Broady, chairman of the Department of Journalism and Public Communications at the University of Alaska, Anchorage, formed an Advisory Council of which Augie was first chairman. The Council, made up of industry representatives from newspaper, radio, TV, and production, was formed to guide Dr. Broady in structuring the academic program to groom professionals for the broadcast market.

Dr. Broady shares Augie's advocacy of hands-on training. As a builder of her own successful department, she shares, too, in Augie's wisdom and enjoyment of putting things together from nothing; called "Alaskan ingenuity," it reflects the resourcefulness of making due with what you have and learning from it. The Department staff has also been prolific in their publication of research and has made recommendations to the state legislature about Alaska telecommunications and the future.

Although satellite service to Alaska was well established, local urban television stations did not share in the rewards of same-day network programming until 1984. All three major network's were content to maintain the status quo in microwave delivery by AT&T. Alaskan stations had campaigned since the early 1970s to correct the delay system of distribution to Alaska, but the networks did not want to commit themselves sooner than necessary to a new technology that would cost a lot of money. Augie had challenged the network delivery system and encouraged a conversion as a member of the CBS Affiliate Satellite Transmission Committee in the late 1960s.

But nothing changed until one day AT&T decided to charge the networks a whole lot more for its service as carrier. Coupled with this was the coming of age of satellite delivery technology—satellite capacity had increased in number and utilization—so the price was right and the time was right to make a change. The networks then instituted a program of distribution; when one network converted, the others followed. Alaskans had long endured delays in television programming but that was now a thing of the past. The only remaining delays were the result of the difference in time zone between Anchorage and New York. That four hour delay Alaskans can live with!

Clear Channel for Alaska's radio airwaves came on

October 25, 1984, the outcome of almost four decades of vigilance on Augie's part. In 1946 Augie had traveled to Washington, D.C. to petition the FCC to continue KFAR's 10,000-watt status granted on a temporary basis for war purposes. (He had met then with Rosel Hyde, a newly appointed FCC commissioner in 1946. Almost forty years later, Rosel celebrated with Augie the resolution of Clear Channel for Alaska. This may have been the longest association in FCC history for the purpose of resolving a single broadcast issue.) Augie's interest in Clear Channel was rekindled with the acquisition of two AM stations, KBYR and KFRB, following the 1964 earthquake.

A Clear Channel license would permit radio stations to go to maximum power. But the rules for licensing higher power, based on studies done in the 1930s in the Lower 48, were prohibitive. One of the Clear Channel rules that affected Alaskan stations was that a clear channel station could not have another station in the United States on that same frequency. Another rule said that a radio signal could not exceed a certain strength at the closest American border, regardless of border or station location.

Augie knew from his experience with short wave reception how far signals would travel here, that Arctic propagation was entirely different, and that the curves used by the FCC for calculating distances that signals would travel were not applicable to Alaska. The Canadians, in fact, were using different curves for determining frequency and coverage compatibility.

It became obvious to Augie that to overcome these FCC restrictions, studies would have to be initiated to document the Arctic propagation phenomenon. Funding for the research, conducted by Dr. Robert Hunsucker of the University of Alaska, Geophysical Institute, came through a federal grant that Senator Stevens helped acquire, and through the sponsorship of the Alaska Public Broadcasting Commission. Dr. Hunsucker, along with Professors Glen Stanley and Robert Merritt, had served as technical advisors to the Governor's Task Force on Telecommunications in the early 1970s when Augie was its chairman.

The initial three-year study, which began in the early 1980s, was later extended to include half of the eleven-year sun spot cycle, because it is sun spot eruptions that affect the magnetic disturbances which influence propagation. Dr. Hunsucker capsulizes the project this way:

> Augie has also been our champion at the Geophysical Institute in fighting to obtain and continue funding for our research on "Medium frequency skywave propagation at high latitudes," which is intended to provide new information to the FCC from which they can make more realistic frequency allocations in the standard AM broadcasting band. This should help rural areas of Alaska to obtain better (interference-free) reception of Alaskan AM stations. Through Augie's influence with Senator Stevens, the FCC has been "continually encouraged" to fund our research, and several miles of red tape have been eliminated (or at least, uncoiled!).

The FCC had also been conducting low altitude studies through their Boulder, Colorado, operations. The data had never been analyzed, so Dr. Hunsucker was also contracted through the Geophysical Institute to analyze this supplemental information.

In 1982 Tom Busch, president of the Alaska Broadcasters Association, was influential in promoting Clear Channel status for Alaska AM radio. The issue became critical in 1982 when the Canadians petitioned for rule changes in their frequency allocations. The threat to Alaska AM stations was imminent. If the petitions were granted, Alaska stations' coverage areas would be reduced to a thirty-mile radius, eliminating interference-free AM radio reception for much of the state.

The "Alaska Day at the FCC" had provided a forum to explain Alaska's unique communication challenges. The significance of Clear Channel resolution had been well defined at the time for both public and commercial stations. With this background and an arsenal of research data, Augie and Tom Busch initiated a petition that was submitted to an enlightened FCC. Championed as well by Senator Stevens, the result two years later was the creation of an entire new category for Alaska Clear Channels, 1-N. Alaska stations were protected from Canadian interference as well as domestic interference in a decision hailed as a remarkable action by the FCC. That was October 24, 1984.

Six weeks later, on December 6, 1984, the FCC issued its final order that the objections filed in 1977 by Alaskans for Better Media (ABM) be denied and that the collective license renewals for NTV stations be granted. In June 1980 KIMO-TV, Central Broadcasting, had settled with ABM and their license renewal was granted the following month. Northern Television's license renewals were also granted, by order of the FCC, on more than one occasion. Each time, however, objections were appealed in court by ABM's Media Access Project Counsel, Andrew Schwartzman. Throughout the process of judgments and appeals, Augie remained steadfast in his commitment to not enter into a settlement agreement with ABM. He chose to defend his license renewals in a lengthy opposition to ABM's voluminous petition, specific to each charge. Finally, through the compelling arguments presented by Leon Knauer and his Washington D.C., legal staff, the outcome was favorable for Augie and Northern Television.

The final irony was that Schwartzman stood in counsel on his own behalf. It was revealed during the proceedings that Schwartzman had no client. Alaskans for Better Media had been dissolved. Court appeals prolonged the ordeal until the final resolution in May 1985, following a long, hard fought battle (seven years of litigation and appeals and $400,000 in legal costs). A quiet victory in the end, perhaps, but one achieved through singularity of purpose and commitment to conscience.

Victories are packaged many ways, and 1985 was gift wrapped with awards. Anchorage Community College chose Augie as the 1985 recipient of its Meritorious Service Award, presented at commencement exercises on May 9, 1985. Endowment of the award was established in 1982 by approval of the University of Alaska Board of Regents as a vehicle to recognize outstanding and exemplary service to the community college. Augie joined previous recipients Mary Hale and ACC electronics instructor Robert Leach.

On May 12, Augie was presented as well with a certificate designating him an Honorary Member of the University of Alaska Alumni Association, "for outstanding contributions to the University of Alaska and its alumni."

The highlight of the Alaska Broadcasters Association Convention in 1985 was the inauguration of the ABA Hall of Fame. A prestigious celebration honored ten inductees, voted on by all Alaska licensees, for their pioneering contributions: Al Bramstedt, Sr., Bob Fleming, Ralph Fondell, Ruben Gaines, Charlie Gray, Bill Harpel, Patty Harpel, Capt Lathrop, Roy Robinson, and Augie Hiebert. The look back at Alaska's broadcast history, along with the presentation of awards and a Hall of Fame ring, made for an emotional evening.

Subsequent Hall of Fame inductees have included Dr. Charles Northrip and Bill Wagner (1986) and Stanton D. Bennett (1987). Augie bestowed Stan's award in a Seattle hospital room, where a few days later, Stan succumbed to his long battle with cancer.

The spring and summer of 1988 Augie was in his element—field testing. He and Pat traveled many miles from Kenai to Talkeetna recording reams of signal strength measurements for KBYR at 1,000 watts in late May, 5,000 watts in late June, and 10,000 watts in August.

The focus of this decade has been on radio because several significant events affecting radio occurred during the 1980s. Television, however, was taking no back seat to radio in the modernization process. Advancements in broadcast technology, coupled with technical and competitive demands, dictated upgrades and integration, especially with the beginning of live satellite broadcasts. In an eight-year period, beginning in 1980, Northern Television replaced and added $3 million of new equipment. Northern Television's entire radio and television operation was upgraded with new studio and news cameras, new transmitters and antennas for KTVA-TV, KTVF-TV, KNIK-FM; and two fully equipped earth stations each in Anchorage and Fairbanks. A new production department with state-of-the-art equipment and facilities was also added in the mid-1980s.

The planning and installation of this equipment was performed by Duane Millsap, director of engineering at Northern Television, Anchorage, his assistant John Antonuk, and their expert staff. Parallel accomplishments were made in Fairbanks by chief engineer Les Secrest, assisted by Bill Tanner and their staff.

As Augie puts it, the wave of the future is already upon us with the rapid advancements in solid state technology and miniaturization to permit more mobile and comprehensive news and sports coverage.

• • •

Augie Hiebert, pioneer Alaskan, continues to ride "full steam" the rails of progress in Alaska telecommunications. He is fueled by the spirit of the Last Frontier, by the people, and by the land. Augie is a man of vision. Someone may someday walk in his footsteps, but no one will ever walk in his shoes. He has given much to Alaska, but most of all he has given himself. And for that we are all the richer.

Augie throws switch for sign on 10,000 watt KCBF,
Formerly KFRB, Faibanks, 1981.

Augie watches as "Bird Bath" is positioned for live TV network satellite reception.

Alaska Broadcaster's Association official Hall of Fame photograph, September 1985.

The occasion of Pat Hiebert's Investiture as a Dame of Malta, April 1988, Washington D.C. Pictured from left are friend Margaret Bryant, Pat and Augie in their official Order of Malta attire, friend and hostess Traude Knauer and Dame Rose Lee.

Augie throwing switch for KBYR radio increased power, June 20, 1988.

Granddaughter Melissa is instructed in field testing procedure as Augie evaluates the strength of KBYR at different and prescribed distances subsequent to increased power capabilities, July 1988.

The broadcast center, August 1988. The story of a broadcast lifetime!

APPENDIX

VIDEO	AUDIO
Bal—KTVA	THOMAS: This is KTVA Channel 11 Anchorage, Alaska
Bal-TITLE "Sign On"	(THEME #1 UP SECS AND UNDER) THOMAS: Good evening this is Fred Thomas welcoming you to KTVA's first telecast "Sign On." Your Master of Ceremonies for "Sign On" is Frank Brink.
L—BRINK	BRINK: At this time you will see one more beginning in Alaska, that of a television service produced for and by Alaskans. To many of you, television will be a completely new experience but as time goes by I'm sure it will become a regular and necessary part of your daily life. It won't be long until you will be talking a new language filled with expressions like "snow," "ghosts," "fringe area," "diffusion," and others having to do with the quality and performance of your TV set and your reception. We

Dolly back
pan and
dolly in to
C.U. of
Hiebert

sincerely hope that your reception will be trouble free at least most of the time. By now you have established that KTVA is telecasting into your home or your place of business. It took much patient planning and devotion to bring about this simple beginning and I'm sure you'd like to meet the man who is chiefly responsible for it, Mr. A. G. Hiebert, president and general Manager of Northern Television.

BEL—
ALASKA FLAG

THOMAS: You have been watching the first official telecast of the Northern Television Corporation Station KTVA. We hope you have enjoyed this introduction to KTVA's Television Service and personnel.

L—BRINK

BRINK: One hundred years from now the citizens of Anchorage will not remember what has happened here at KTVA on this 11th day of December 1953. That it was KTVA's first official telecast will be of little concern to them: That it presented several beginnings in television for Anchorage, Alaska will not be recalled: That these people on our opening telecast took a moment out of their lives to participate with the staff of KTVA in launching its daily service to Alaskans will not be particularly important in the 21st century. However, there will be something begun here today which will be important to them, something with which the people of 2053 will be concerned and with which they will have to deal in their own time. It is the question of whether or not KTVA maintains its integrity as a public servant, its support of civic institutions, civic benefits, local business, its loyalty to Alaska and unfailing allegiance to the United States. This, the Anchorage citizens of 2053 will be vitally concerned with, for this will directly effect them and their way of life. With this in mind, KTVA dedicates itself to uphold and contribute to these ideals so that when those present here today have passed from the scene, what KTVA has done for Alaska may be considered one more contribution to the development, maturity, and freedom so many have come here to find.

STATEMENT PREPARED FOR
PUBLIC SERVICE COMMISSION
RCA ALASCOM HEARINGS
June 10, 1970
A. G. Hiebert

My comments to the Public Service Commission are directed primarily toward the broad telecommunications horizon, wherein Alaska has the unique opportunity to guide its own destiny into the capabilities of space age telecommunications, embracing known technological concepts which offer the promise of a twenty-first-century communications system with all the benefits which have not been available in the past.

Alaska's present terrestrial communications system, serving only a portion of Alaska, is the backbone of what should be considered only a transitional short-term means of communicating within the boundaries of the state and to distant points in much the same manner as we have experienced during the past few years. It can be improved and expanded to serve additional areas where needs develop. There are many points within Alaska where this terrestrial link is practical and capable of providing an adequate service for some time to come.

The urgency of the moment is for the Alaska Public Service Commission to view the existing system in proper perspective, and to preserve and safeguard the options for its integration into a new and proven technology which will serve with equal versatility and quality every corner of the State of Alaska and all its people.

Satellite communications offer the bright promise to accomplish the philosophy and infinite benefits to a total Alaskan Telecommunications System. A satellite—in geostationary orbit 22,300 miles distant from the earth—will illuminate every Alaskan city and village, offering equal opportunity for all Alaskans to communicate in whatever mode of transmission suits their needs and requirements. The sociological, economic, and educational benefits are obvious and need no amplification here.

Alaska has an uncommon opportunity; the Alaska Public Service Commission bears an unparalleled responsibility to at once guide and protect the destiny of what can become the model telecommunications system of the world. The economic, social, technological factors are all present—the timing is perfect—the scenario can be, and must be written to provide for adequate communications wherever there are Alaskans who need to communicate within our state. Someone must speak for the isolated villages; someone must be concerned about opening the window on the world educationally to those who have been exposed by our society to the urban way of life, and now must learn to cope with it. Someone with policy making powers and judicial wisdom must care about Alaskans outside the mainstream of advantages we take for granted. The opportunity to learn, ranging from the elementary "Sesame Street" to simple hygiene which will help stretch the rural Alaskan's span of life to national standards, must be made available to these people where they live. Reference is made to a review of the role telecommunications can play in Alaska which was written for the Brookings Institution seminar held in Anchorage last November and December. Quotations are primarily from guest speakers who defined the issues and related the potential solutions to the Brookings conferees. This "Anatomy of Alaska's Telecommunications Requirements" is attached as part of my comments.

Reference is also made to an address to the Alaska Broadcasters Association annual conference in Juneau, May

25, 1970, by Lieutenant General Robert G. Ruegg, Commander-in-Chief, Alaskan Command. General Ruegg, as Chairman of the Federal Field Committee Communications Working Group, defined in crystal-clear terms the critical part the military establishment might well play as a communications user throughout Alaska, when a modern system is available to first supplement and then replace the overloaded, obsolete, and inadequate White Alice System. This observation relates to the large segment of the military communications system which does not include the Alaska Communications System portion being offered for sale. I have attached the full text of General Ruegg's highly significant comments and request that they be made part of the record of these proceedings.

This statement before the Alaska Public Service Commission is really an appeal to view the distant telecommunications horizon with a bold and imaginative eye. Visualize the significance of an ultra-modern concept linking all of Alaska into one integrated system which can accommodate every mode of communication now known to man, and still be flexible to encompass future developments. Then, in your deliberations, as you weigh the vast quantities of evidence presented to you, please preserve for Alaska all of the options the state must have to be responsive to future system concepts, rate-making procedures, and regulatory policies which will encourage and protect communications in rural, lightly populated areas,and also preserve the state's future prerogatives through your regulatory control.

The expertise to accomplish the ultimate Alaskan telecommunications concept and system design is readily available. The time to accomplish it is in the critical near future, during the transitional phase when the ACS portion of the military system is transferred to private enterprise. The assurance that this vital door to the communications future of Alaska be left open to accommodate a continued and effective state response to future needs and requirements is a challenging Public Service Commission responsibility. Thank you for the opportunity to express my views.

KTVA - CBS NEWS RELEASE
FEBRUARY 24, 1971 - 4:30 PM

SATELLITE TELEVISION COVERAGE OF THE DEPARTMENT OF INTERIOR'S ENVIRONMENTAL HEARINGS ON THE TRANS-ALASKA PIPELINE WAS AIRED TONIGHT IN THE LOWER 48 STATES. THE BROADCAST WAS THE FIRST SUCCESSFUL COMMERCIAL SATELLITE TRANSMISSION GOING SOUTH FROM ALASKA.

THE COVERAGE AIRED FROM SYDNEY LAWRENCE AUDITORIUM, WAS TRANSMITTED THROUGH THE BROADCAST CENTER-KTVA TO THE BARTLETT EARTH STATION AT TALKEETNA, THEN TO THE SATELLITE, AND RECEIVED AT THE COLUMBIA BROADCASTING SYSTEM'S STUDIOS IN NEW YORK.

THE COLOR PICTURE AND SOUND QUALITY WERE SUPERIOR, ACCORDING TO CBS NEWS IN NEW YORK. THE FIVE MINUTE REPORT ON THE PIPELINE HEARINGS WAS PART OF THE CBS EVENING NEWS WITH WALTER CRONKITE, AIRED NATIONALLY.

"TODAY ALASKANS CAN BE PROUD THAT A MAJOR NEWS EVENT HAPPENING IN THEIR STATE WAS SEEN BY MILLIONS ELSEWHERE ON A SAME-DAY BASIS," ACCORDING TO A. G. HIEBERT, PRESIDENT OF NORTHERN TELEVISION, INCORPORATED. PREVIOUSLY, TELEVISION NETWORK FILM CREWS HAD TO SHOOT FOOTAGE HERE, AND SHIP IT SOUTH FOR BROADCAST. THE DELAY WAS USUALLY 24 HOURS OR MORE. IT WAS ONLY A MATTER OF MINUTES FROM THE TIME TESTIMONY WAS PRESENTED AT THE HEARINGS, UNTIL IT WAS SEEN ACROSS THE COUNTRY.

CBS NEWS WEST COAST BUREAU MANAGER JOHN HARRIS WAS IN ANCHORAGE TO COORDINATE THE NETWORK'S COVERAGE. "BROADCASTS LIKE THIS, PERHAPS MORE THAN ANYTHING ELSE, WILL BRING THE VIEWS OF ALASKANS QUICKLY AND CLEARLY TO THE REST OF THE COUNTRY. IN A REAL SENSE, IN TELEVISION NEWS, ALASKA IS NOW EQUAL TO THE OTHER 49 STATES," HARRIS SAID.

THE COVERAGE WAS AIRED AS A FIVE MINUTE SEGMENT OF THE CRONKITE NEWS. CBS NEWS CORRESPONDENT TERRY DRINKWATER REPORTED FROM HERE FOR HIS NETWORK. "WITHOUT THE RATHER CONSIDERABLE NEWS CAPABILITY AND TECHNICAL COMPETENCE OF THE KTVA STAFF, THE COMPLEX TRANSMISSION WOULD NOT HAVE WORKED," ACCORDING TO DRINKWATER.

"THE TRANS-ALASKA PIPELINE CONTROVERSY IS OF VITAL INTEREST IN THE LOWER 48 AS WELL AS HERE. THE DEBATE ON THE SUBJECT IS REALLY A NATIONAL ONE. BUT WHAT ALASKANS HAVE TO SAY IS DOUBLY IMPORTANT. THAT IS WHY THIS SATELLITE FEED FROM KTVA TO CBS WAS HIGHLY SIGNIFICANT FROM THE NEWS STANDPOINT," DRINKWATER SAID.

THE ENTIRE CBS FEED WAS HANDLED BY KTVA ENGINEERS, UNDER THE DIRECTION OF JEFF BOWDEN AND MEL SATHER.

THE COLOR TRANSMISSION FROM KTVA TO THE REST OF THE COUNTRY WAS "BRILLIANTLY CLEAR," ACCORDING TO PETE HERFORD, THE NEW YORK CBS NEWS CRONKITE PRODUCER, WHO RECEIVED THE FEED FROM ANCHORAGE. HERFORD WILL BE REMEMBERED HERE AS

A FORMER KTVA STAFFER HIMSELF. TWELVE YEARS AGO HE WAS AMONG THE PIONEERS IN ALASKA TELEVISION. "YOU'VE COME A LONG WAY FROM THOSE PRIMITIVE DAYS. I COULD HARDLY BELIEVE IT," HERFORD SAID WHEN HE SAW THE FEED.

NOW, WITH THE FEED FROM ALASKA TODAY ALL 50 STATES ARE ABLE TO SEE THE NEWS, LIVE AND DIRECT, FROM EACH AREA.

EDITORIAL BY A. G. HIEBERT
12/19/77

FELLOW ALASKANS; I HAVE BEEN A BROADCASTER IN
ALASKA FOR MORE THAN 38 YEARS, AND THIS IS THE
FIRST TIME I HAVE CHOSEN, ON A PERSONAL BASIS, TO
EDITORIALIZE. I WAS OUT OF THE STATE RECENTLY
WHEN I FIRST HEARD THAT A STRONG PROTEST HAD
BEEN FILED WITH THE FEDERAL COMMUNICATIONS
COMMISSION AGAINST THE PROPOSED SALE OF A
COMPETITOR OF MINE, MIDNIGHT SUN BROADCASTERS,
INCORPORATED. WITH THE FACTS NOW AVAILABLE TO
ME, I WANT TO SHARE WITH YOU MY OPINIONS OF THIS
ACTION, WHICH I VIEW PERSONALLY AND
PROFESSIONALLY AS AN ALARMING INVASION OF FAIR
PLAY, AS WELL AS THE RIGHTS OF THE DISTINGUISHED
BROADCASTER AND HIS COMPANY, TO CONDUCT
BUSINESS IN AN HONEST AND FORTHRIGHT MANNER.
MR. ALVIN O. BRAMSTEDT, PRESIDENT OF MIDNIGHT SUN
BROADCASTERS, INCORPORATED, IS A COMPETITOR OF
MINE. WE COMPETE VIGOROUSLY FOR RADIO AND
TELEVISION ADVERTISING REVENUE IN BOTH
ANCHORAGE AND FAIRBANKS, AND WE COMPETE FOR
LISTENERS AND VIEWERS THROUGH PROGRAMMING ON
OUR MEDIA. WE DO THIS IN THE SPIRIT OF FREE
ENTERPRISE—THE AMERICAN WAY. THE ADVERTISING
DOLLARS WE ATTRACT TO OPERATE OUR RADIO AND TV
STATIONS ALLOWS US TO BRING FREE BROADCASTING TO
ALASKA—AT NO COST TO THE TAXPAYER OR HOME
OWNER, AND AVAILABLE TO ALL WHO CAN AFFORD TO
BUY A RADIO OR TV SET. BOTH OF US HAVE PIONEERED
IN THE DEVELOPMENT OF ALASKAN MEDIA, AND WE
BOTH HAVE EXPERIENCED MANY YEARS OF SEVERE
FINANCIAL STRUGGLES TO ACCOMPLISH OUR GOAL FOR

A FREE MEDIA AS AN ENTERTAINMENT AND PUBLIC SERVICE BENEFIT TO URBAN AND RURAL ALASKANS ALIKE.

WHY, THEN, SHOULD A STRONG ROADBLOCK, BY NEWLY ORGANIZED FORCES WITHIN THE STATE OF ALASKA, BE THROWN IN THE WAY OF A MAN AND HIS COMPANY, WHEN HE WISHES TO RETIRE AND SELL THAT BUSINESS TO FINANCIALLY STABLE AND COMPETENT BUYERS? I ASK YOU TO DRAW YOUR OWN CONCLUSIONS TO THAT QUESTION.

LET ME ADDRESS THE SUBJECT OF WHY MR. AL BRAMSTEDT, KNOWN TO ALL AS "BRAM," SHOULD BE ALLOWED TO TRANSFER OWNERSHIP OF HIS COMPANY WITH NO OPPOSITION AT ALL AT THE FCC. AS A BROADCASTER, AND BUSINESSMAN, WHO WILL HAVE CONTRIBUTED HIS BEST TO ALASKA FOR 38 YEARS NEXT MONTH, BRAM HAS EARNED THE RIGHT TO RELINQUISH THE REINS TO COMPETENT BUYERS. TRUE, IN THE FEDERALLY REGULATED MEDIA BUSINESS, A SELLER AND A BUYER MUST BOTH APPLY FOR PERMISSION TO DO THIS, SO THAT THE FCC CAN APPROVE, ON THE MERIT OF THE TRANSACTION, IN THE PUBLIC INTEREST. THE PROPOSED BUYERS OF MIDNIGHT SUN BROADCASTERS, INCORPORATED CONSIST OF A MAJORITY OF WELL KNOWN LOCAL BUSINESSMEN, WHO THROUGH MANY HEARS, HAVE ALSO DEMONSTRATED THEIR INTEGRITY AND ABILITY TO GROW AND DEVELOP IN THIS STATE, AND A HIGHLY RESPECTED AND ASTUTE BROADCASTER, MR. KEN HATCH OF SEATTLE, WASHINGTON, WITH EXPERIENCE AND ABILITIES WELL KNOWN IN OUR INDUSTRY, WHO IS SLATED TO MANAGE THE COMPANY AFTER TRANSFER OF OWNERSHIP. THERE IS NO SHRED

OF EVIDENCE THAT THE BUYERS CANNOT CARRY ON THE PUBLIC SERVICE TRADITIONS OF BRAM AND HIS ASSOCIATES. TO THE CONTRARY, THEY HAVE THE STABILITY, INTEGRITY, THE BUSINESS ABILITY AND THE FINANCIAL RESOURCES TO KEEP PACE WITH GROWING ALASKA, TO IMPROVE THESE MEDIA FACILITIES AS TIME GOES BY. AND TO SERVE AND REPRESENT ALL FACETS OF THE ALASKAN PUBLIC, IN AN OUTSTANDING PROFESSIONAL, AND COMMUNITY SERVICE MANNER. TO ME, AS I'M SURE IT IS TO ANY BUSINESS OR PROFESSIONAL PERSON, IT IS FUNDAMENTAL FAIR PLAY TO ALLOW A WILLING SELLER TO TRANSACT BUSINESS WITH A WILLING BUYER.

I THINK YOU SHOULD KNOW THERE IS ANOTHER CONSIDERATION WHICH I FEEL COMPELLED TO DIVULGE TO YOU, AND I TRUST I DON'T EMBARRASS BRAM BY DOING SO. AT STAKE IS THE HEALTH OF A COURAGEOUS MAN. SINCE 1946 BRAM HAS CONTINUED HIS ROLE AS A LEADING BROADCASTER IN ALASKA, FIGHTING OFF THE RAVAGES OF CRIPPLING ARTHRITIS. FOR 31 YEARS IT HAS BEEN AN ALMOST IMPOSSIBLE EFFORT FOR HIM TO MOVE MUCH LESS TO WORK AT THE DEMANDING JOB OF RUNNING A BROADCASTING BUSINESS. HE HAS HAD PAINFUL AND DEBILITATING OPERATIONS—BOTH HIPS HAVE BEEN REMOVED—BOTH KNEES HAVE BEEN REMOVED AND REPLACED BY ARTIFICIAL JOINTS—IN AN EFFORT TO RESTORE MOBILITY. THESE OPERATIONS HAVE BEEN ONLY PARTIALLY SUCCESSFUL. HAS BRAM EARNED THE RIGHT TO SELL HIS BUSINESS AND RETIRE, IN PART, TO A MORE COMFORTABLE CLIMATE IF HE SO DESIRES?

IF YOU AGREE WITH ME THAT HE HAS, AND WISH TO

MAKE YOUR VIEWS KNOWN WHERE THEY WILL COUNT THE MOST, I URGE YOU TO WRITE TO THE FEDERAL COMMUNICATIONS COMMISSION, WASHINGTON, D.C. AND EXPRESS YOUR OPINIONS. WASHINGTON IS 3,000 MILES AWAY, AND THE CONSCIENCE OF ALASKANS CAN BE EXPRESSED MOST EFFECTIVELY IF STATED IN WRITING TO THE AGENCY WHOSE DECISION IT WILL BE TO GRANT THE TRANSFER OF OWNERSHIP. ADDRESS YOUR LETTERS TO THE FEDERAL COMMUNICATIONS COMMISSION, 1919 "M" STREET, N.W., WASHINGTON D.C., 20554. AS ONE ALASKAN TO ANOTHER—THANK YOU.